Believing Three Ways in One God

Believing Three Ways in One God

A Reading of the Apostles' Creed

Nicholas Lash

UNIVERSITY OF NOTRE DAME PRESS

NOTRE DAME   LONDON

First published in the United States in 1993 by
University of Notre Dame Press
Notre Dame, Indiana 46556
All Rights Reserved

Published by SCM Press Ltd,
26–30 Tottenham Road, London N1 4BZ

Library of Congress Cataloging-in-Publication Data

Lash, Nicholas.
    Believing three ways in one God : a reading of the
Apostles' Creed / Nicholas Lash.
        p.   cm.
    Includes bibliographical references.
    ISBN 0-268-00691-1
    1. Apostles' Creed.   I. Title.
    BT993.2.L37   1993
238'.11—dc20   92-33909
                                                CIP

Manufactured in Great Britain

Contents

Preface

I   Amen   1

II   Short Words and Endless Learning   4

1. The way things hang together   4
2. Declaration and investigation   7
3. Reading Creeds   11
4. Why the Apostles' creed?   13

III   Believing in God   17

1. Believing   17
2. Believing in God   19
3. Believing in one God   22
4. How many articles?   25
5. Believing three ways in one God   30

IV   Producing   34

1. Creating   35
2. Sonship   42
    '... what he sees the Father doing'   47
3. Harmony   49

V   Appearing   55

1. Utterance   64
2. Delight   73
3. Speaking   79

VI   Peacemaking   83

1. Donation   91
2. Giving   106
3. Forgiving   111

VII   Gardening   121

Notes   125

Preface

This book is written for people educated in every area of their life and work except theology who say the Creed each Sunday and sometimes wonder what they mean. My hope is that, rather than being read once, from start to finish, and then put back upon the shelf, it will be *used* – as an aid to group discussion, for example, and, perhaps, to prayer.

There is no shortage of small books about the Creed, but none of those with which I am familiar takes seriously enough its trinitarian character. If this book works the way I hope it will, it will bring its readers to a fresh sense of the way all things hang together in relation to the mystery that we confess as Father, Son and Spirit.

I could not have written it without the generous hospitality of the University of Notre Dame, where we spent the school year 1991–1992. My thanks, especially, to Lawrence Cunningham, bearing with such grace the burdens of the chairmanship of the Theology Department, to Michael Buckley, David Burrell and Michael Himes, and to the class of 'theology majors' who discussed each chapter with me. At least as important as the academic context of the university, however, was the 'space' (as Philip Corbett would say) provided by the community of St. Augustine's in South Bend.

To John Bowden and James Langford, and their colleagues at (respectively) SCM Press and the University of Notre Dame Press, my deep appreciation for their encouragement and care during the process of production.

My wife's patience and kindness as a critic never ceases to amaze me, and I am especially grateful to her for suggesting that the book should set out from 'Amen'.

Nicholas Lash

Notre Dame
May 1992

For
the parish community of Saint Augustine's,
Washington Avenue, South Bend, Indiana

I

Amen

'Amen' should surely come, not at the beginning, but at the end? 'Amen' comes after, not before, a text, announcement, testimony or pledge. Moses and the priests said to all Israel: 'Keep silence and hear, O Israel: this day you have become the people of the Lord your God. You shall therefore obey the voice of the Lord your God, keeping his commandments and his statutes, which I command you this day.' And Moses ordered that, after the proclamation of each anathema on those who broke these statutes and commandments, 'all the people shall answer and say, "Amen"'.[1]

'Amen' comes after, and the context of its utterance is usually a solemn act of worship. It is a people-binding act, a pledge of solidarity with the purposes and promises of God. Thus when Nehemiah, furious to discover that the nobles and officials were exacting interest and selling their own people into slavery, made them swear an oath to restore the property and repay the taxes which they had exacted, 'all the assembly said "Amen" and praised the Lord. And the people did as they had promised'.[2]

'Amen' comes after and, in the end, all justice done and promises secured, the note of celebration, never quite absent from its use, rings out victorious without the sterner tones of duty to be done. 'After this I heard what seemed to be the mighty voice of a great multitude in heaven, crying, "Alleluia! Salvation and glory and power belong to our God, for his judgments are true and just" ... And the twenty-four elders and the four living creatures fell down and worshipped God who is seated on the throne, saying "Amen, Alleluia"!'[3]

'Amen', like 'Alleluia', is, in the right context, one of those rare words which says almost everything we need to say. Of course, in order to furnish such a context, we need endlessly to labour at improving the quality of our performance. As we work to act a little less clumsily, less inhumanly, less thoughtlessly; to speak a little less ignorantly, less dishonestly, less inattentively, there is always much to say and even more to do. Only God speaks one Word which says everything, which makes and heals the world.

Given the richness and complexity of things, the permanence of change, the fragmentariness of our understanding, it is hardly surprising that great texts and treatises – on physics and philosophy, on thermodynamics and theology, on literature and law – should grow and multiply and fill the earth (or, at least, its libraries). It sometimes seems that there is not, nor can there ever be, in principle, an end in sight: a time to say 'Amen'.

'Amen' comes after, and yet the incompleteness of our understanding, the endless labour of interpretation, does not entitle us indefinitely to postpone its utterance. We are even now required (and therefore must be able) to say quite simply everything we need to say. Different peoples, different communities construct over time, have different abbreviations, forms of sound words, declarations of identity or independence, acknowledgments of where they stand. For the Christian, pride of place amongst such formulas is taken by the Creed.

'Amen' comes after, but nonetheless we may begin with it because what it comes after is everything that went before. Theologians spend much time arguing where they should *begin*. This is a largely futile exercise because, if one thing is certain in this life, it is that none of us begins at the beginning. We find ourselves somewhere, discover something of what went before, of how things went in order to bring about the way they are. Growing up is largely a matter of learning to take bearings. A more fruitful question than 'Where should we begin?' would almost always be 'Where, then, do we stand?'.

'Amen' comes after, even when we begin with it, because responsibly to say 'Amen' demands some prior understanding on our part. How, Paul asked rhetorically of those whose speaking in tongues was uninterpreted, can anyone 'say the "Amen" to your thanksgiving when he does not know what you are saying?'.[4] 'Amen' uttered thoughtlessly is not an act of faith but idle chatter, and this is intolerable paradox because the word, in Hebrew, is one of a cluster from a root which signifies reliability, integrity and truth.

Our 'Amen' comes after, even when (as here) we set it at the start, because our utterance of it is acknowledgment of God's 'Amen', which always goes before. The recognition of God's integrity or truthfulness, unswerving faithfulness in execution of his promises, is so central to Judaism's faith that 'Amen' may almost be taken as a name for God. We might miss this when we read, in the sixty-fifth chapter of Isaiah, that 'he who takes an oath in the land shall swear by the God of truth', but the Hebrew here, if rendered literally, would be 'by the God Amen'. And, in what is perhaps an echo of this text, John is instructed: 'to the angel of the church in Laodicea write: "The words of the Amen, the faithful and true witness, the beginning of God's creation".'[5]

We can say 'Yes', then, can confess 'Amen', can pledge ourselves to continue the work that is begun, conclude that, in the end, all shall be well, because, from the beginning, there is only 'Yes' in God. 'For the Son of God, Jesus Christ, whom we preached among you ... was not Yes or No; but in him it is always Yes. For all the promises of God find their Yes in him. That is why we utter the Amen through him, to the glory of God ... [who] has put his seal upon us and given us his Spirit in our hearts as a guarantee.'[6]

My intention, in this book, is simply to offer a reading of the Apostles' Creed which will (I hope) help those who use it to some deeper understanding of the words they say. And I shall try to show that to deepen understanding of *these* words is to grow in knowledge of ourselves, each other, and the world, and of the mystery of God. In that passage from Paul's second letter to the church at Corinth we can discern already, as early as the sixth decade of the Christian era, the contours of the Creed, the Christian acknowledgment of God's Amen, confession of faith in Father, Son and Spirit, testimony that, from the beginning to the end, Alpha to Omega, the first word and the last, and all that goes between, is 'Yes': 'Amen'.

II

Short Words and Endless Learning

1. The way things hang together

Without some sense of how things hang together we get lost, go mad, or die. But different things hang together differently, are differently organized, constructed, unified, made one. Consider what it is that makes 'one' catalogue, one sea-slug, or one solar system; one rookery, one rope, one war, one human individual; one possibility, one city, one story, or one world. My interest, at this point, is in the oneness of the Creed; in how that hangs together, and in what the implications of its oneness are for our understanding of the oneness or identity or each of us, of Christianity, the human race, the world, and God. A tall order for a short chapter!

In some cultures, it has seemed evident that everything does hang together in some way, can be brought under some one appropriate description, grasped in some single explanatory system, or constitute one single story with a single plot and a beginning, a middle and an end. Today, in Western culture, we lack such confidence. We have become increasingly aware, not merely of how fragmentary is our understanding of the confusing and confused complexity of things, how shaped by place and time and circumstance, how distorted by filters of fear and prejudice and power; but also of how different different people are – their memories, their dreams, their suffering – and how interminable the web of possibilities woven in the telling of new tales, the outcome of new experiences, the making of new enemies and friends.

And yet, it is not only scientists in search of ever more comprehensive unifying theories of the world who still proceed, in practice, as if things, after all, did hang together in some way. Each of us has some account to give of who we are, and how things came to be the way they are, and where the world is going. Moreover, whether 'we' be taken to refer to each of us as individuals, or to our tribe, or class, or gender, our nation or profession, or to the human race, we do not, in practice, act as if we took the tales we tell of how things hang together to be only true 'for us'.

Whoever we are, we share a common human nature. But what does this entail? What makes our nature 'one'? What kind of oneness does the human race enjoy? Biological oneness, for a start, in that some animals, and only those, are properly described as human in virtue of belonging to a single species. But genetic solidarity, as we might call it, is not enough to warrant the claim that all human beings share one common nature. Human animals do not only breed, feed and make social arrangements (although they do, in common with other species, do all these things). We also tell stories and dream dreams, consider alternatives and make plans for the future. In other words, human culture, woven from the meanings and values that inform our ways of life, *forms part of human nature*. Therefore, the unity of human nature requires that all members of the species share a common culture: a common life, responsibility and understanding, a common memory and a common hope. And this, for the most part, we so far fail to do. It follows that the oneness or unity of human nature, the way *this* species hangs together, is far from being merely a biological datum. It is also a permanent ethical task and political responsibility. We share one nature in the measure that we are one people, members of one another.

If I were asked how I know that this is so, I should say that I have learned it, and learned it (in fact) within the Christian tradition. And yet, my sketch (so far) of human unity is an open invitation for others to consider, whatever their beliefs or background; it makes no appeal to privileged or secret information to which only Christian faith supposedly gives access. Moreover, in order thus to understand the way things hang together – or fail to do so – in the human world, it is by no means necessary to suffer from the illusion that there is some universal viewpoint, situated nowhere and inhabited by no one in particular, from which questions of unity and difference can be contemplated. Thus, cultural imperialism 'sees' that we are all the same (or must be made to be so, if we are to rise above the darkness of barbarian error), while relativism 'sees' that we are simply different. None of us, in fact, is that far-sighted. We see what we can, from where we are. Feeling our way forward in the dark, seeking to get our bearings, what is required of us is attentiveness, patience and the willingness to learn.

Both imperialism and relativism take an easier option, surrendering the requirements continually to test all stories, the need to be self-critical, genuinely attentive to ways of interpreting and acting out the world, to habits of inference, evaluation and imagination, significantly different from one's own. Even if we lack time or opportunity, energy or courage, to subject our convictions concerning how things hang together to rigorous and detailed scrutiny, few of us (I think) would gladly live or freely die for what we knew to be illusion. All tales need testing.

The most difficult tales to test are not those that we know ourselves to tell as tales, but those that we inhabit. There is, in Western thought, a tension at least as old as Plato between 'myth' and theory (that is: explanation warranted according to accepted rules of evidence and argument). According to most versions of this story, myth comes off badly – as uncontrollable, unwarrantable, suspect of untruth. I intend, so far as possible, to take 'myth', neutrally, to refer to those comprehensive, self-contained narrations of the world within which and according to whose rhythms people live their lives, execute their projects, sustain the ambition and the terror of their dreams. It is this mythic use of narrative I have in mind when speaking of 'the tales that we inhabit'. In the measure that such tales are put to other uses – by making them, for instance, specimens in the laboratory of the literary critic or the anthropologist – they may, of course, be tested by such devices and criteria as we have to hand. But these criteria will then draw their authority, in turn, from some other narrative metaphysic or (in my sense) myth.

Christianity has, from the beginning and with very varying success, sought to have it both ways: to dwell within its myth and yet to set high store by the effort to subject that myth to critical examination. The classic formulation has been *'fides quaerens intellectum'*, faith in search of understanding (understanding *what*, we shall consider in due course).

Christianity finds its myth in Scripture and distils it in the Creed. We shall need to discuss this way of putting it and also to consider whether it implies that the Creed is, itself, a narrative. For the time being, it is enough to make the general point that the oneness or identity of Christian faith, the way things hang together in the Christian scheme of things, has more in common with the oneness of a story with a single plot than with the oneness of a catalogue or list of objects of belief. This might seem so obvious as hardly to need mentioning were it not for the fact that (as we shall see) it has often been supposed that the objects of Christian faith are multiple, and that the Creed contains, as it were, a sample – unified only by the fact that, in every case, God's authority is their sole sufficient ground of credibility – of the more important items in the store!

All tales need testing, but critical scrutiny of the tales that we inhabit, while drawing its criteria from the narratives themselves, first focusses on the ethos, way of life, or project which is shaped and generated by the tale. A cyclical process, to be sure, but by no means necessarily therefore 'vicious' or unfruitful – any more than any other practice of interpretation.

The creeds were shaped by controversy and, as we shall see, their very form is such as to furnish a pattern of self-correction or restraint upon the range of their misuse. The way things hang together, in the Christian scheme of things, is through this ceaseless labour of mutual correction. This may seem a restless or exhausting kind of unity and yet, as we proceed, I shall suggest that it is better seen as the unending and usually discordant labour of people learning to make music, to move closer to the harmony of God, in whom alone all things hold still.

2. Declaration and investigation

Creeds are short texts, easily memorized. But what kind of texts are they, which is to say: how are they best used? Already, the context in which I raise this question indicates the first step towards an answer. Creeds serve to sustain the identity and oneness of the

Christian church in obedience to the One confessed as God and in service of the oneness of the world and of the human race.

With this emphasis on unity in mind, it should be pointed out that what the Creed is not is a list of theses, a catalogue of chapter headings for a textbook of theology. Items in an encyclopaedia or catalogue are juxtaposed, whereas the elements which constitute the Creed are hinged together or, as we say, 'articulated'. Creeds are, moreover, acts of worship and the primary occasions of their use are, accordingly, liturgical. Thus, for example, though baptism is mentioned, the eucharist (surely the occasion on which most Christians most regularly use the creed) is not, although no catechism or handbook of theology could fail to include some treatment of eucharistic doctrine.

What the Scriptures say at length, the Creed says briefly. Something like this has been said in almost every century of the Christian era. Origen already made the point, inspired by a quotation from Isaiah in the ninth chapter of Paul's letter to the Romans which, in the Douai version, reads: '"For he shall finish his word, and cut it short in justice; because a *short word* shall the Lord make upon the earth."'[1]

We are less innocent of the Hebrew text behind the Greek than Origen and Jerome (whose Latin, like that of Origen's translator, had '*verbum breviatum*'), and the modern translations rather spoil the fun: '"for the Lord will execute his sentence upon the earth with vigour and despatch"'.[2] Yet Origen's version is, perhaps, a happy accident. A sentence *is* a 'short word', and the judical connotation ('passing sentence') may remind us that, in our uses of the Creed, we are giving testimony, bearing witness, to the sentence passed by God upon the world: the sentence of forgiveness, God's 'Amen'.

'We hold these truths . . . .' The creeds are acts of worship, public acts of prayer. Within the context or the climate of this, their primary use, they are also the declaration, acknowledged by the community as communally authoritative, of identity-sustaining rules of discourse and behaviour governing Christian uses of the word 'God'. In this sense, then, their function is doctrinal.

'Doctrine' is not, these days, an easy word to use. Like 'dogma', it has overtones of meanings arbitrarily arrived at and hetero-nomously imposed. To describe the Creed as doctrine, therefore, risks losing sight both of the deeply personal, self-involving nature of its proper use, and also of the endless, painstaking, and conflictual labour which necessarily characterizes its interpretation. Let me take these two points in turn.

In the first place, if credal confession is the declaration of identity-sustaining rules of discourse and behaviour governing Christian uses of the word 'God', then creeds cannot be used vicariously. The Creed does not say what someone else believes but what I (or we) believe. It does not simply say where the *world* comes from and where it is being brought, but where I come from and hope to go. If it is a story, then, it is not only the story of the world, but is also autobiographical in character. It is profoundly personal testimony, or it is misused.

In the second place, however, the task of making sense of what we say is endless. And the tension between the resoluteness, the firmness of our declaration, on the one hand, and, on the other, the tentativeness, the attentiveness, with which we seek – in every different circumstance – some proper understanding and application of the mystery in which we move, is indispensable to the integrity of our interpretation. (This is no esoteric doctrine, only applicable to our uses of the creed, for something similar is true of all pledges and proclamations, all 'confessions', all declarations of loyalty and love, in our unfinished and uncertain world – the difference being, of course, that God, the object of our credal faith, remains unkown whereas the world is merely complicated and bewildering.)

What the Scriptures say at length, the Creed says briefly. The Creed does not seek, in Scripture, for warrants or for 'proof', but for intelligibility. If we want to find out what it *means* to confess God as 'creator' or Jesus as God's 'son', then the first place to which we turn is Scripture. But, of course, the interpretation of Scripture is as endless as the diversity of circumstances in which it is read, and of the cultures and occasions which governed its production. In other words, against the tendency of some Christians to say: 'But we know what Scripture means; we find that in the Creed' (and may, therefore, leave the Bible safely closed), I want to emphasize that we only discover the meaning of the Creed in the measure that the Bible stays an open book.

It might, however, be objected that my stress upon the endless-
ness of making sense, upon the labour of interpretation, the un-
avoidability of continuous interpretative disagreement, is out of
place because the truth in question has been definitively given, once
for all revealed, by God. This is an issue to which we shall return,
not least when considering what it means to say God 'speaks'.
Nevertheless, this question of revelation is too fundamental not to
call for some preliminary remarks, however brief.

The legacy of the Enlightenment left us with what we might call a
crisis of docility. Unless we have the courage to work things out for
ourselves, to take as true only that which we have personally
ascertained or, perhaps, invented, then meanings and values,
descriptions and instructions, imposed by other people, feeding
other people's power, will inhibit and enslave us, bind us into fables
and falsehoods from the past. Even God's truth, perhaps especially
God's truth, is no exception to this rule. Only slaves and children
should be teachable, or docile.

The Enlightenment, in other words, tended to treat teaching and
discovery as antithetical activities. Teaching is what we take from
other people and is, therefore, at best unreliable and, at worst,
degrading; truth is what we find out for ourselves.

But this antithesis is most unreal. Admittedly, we only know as
true what we have ascertained, established, worked out to be so.
But that is how we learn – 'doctor' and 'disciple' do, after all, have a
common root. Good teachers understand this: they know that truth
imposed, and not elicited, is most ill-learned. Good teaching is
respectful of those taught.

And, on the other side, of course, not everything that we suppose, come up with, speculate, or put together, works out well. Our
projects and our arguments collapse, interpretations fail, and (if we
are powerful enough) our freewheeling fantasies crush other people
and the silent world beneath their wheels.

Good learning calls, no less than teaching does, for courtesy,
respect, a kind of reverence: for facts and people, evidence and
argument, for climates of speech and patterns of behaviour different from our own. Watchfulness is, indeed, in order, but endless
suspicion and mistrust are not. There are affinities between the
courtesy, the delicacy of attentiveness, required for friendship; the

single-minded passionate disinterestedness without which no good scholarly or scientific work is done; and the contemplativity which strains, without credulity, to listen for the voice of God – who does not shout.

3. *Reading creeds*

The ancient creeds were put together, many centuries ago, in a world so different from our own that most of us have really no idea what made those people 'tick', or how they handled the tales that they indwelt. And today, in spite of the extent to which the whole system or structure of the world has come to form – politically and economically – one large complex fact, one artefact, one single outcome of human energy and avarice and ingenuity, there is no single culture, no common set of meanings, values, or imaginative possibilities, which human beings inhabit. How, then, might all of us confess the faith today and know it to be still the same?

There seem to be four strategies for dealing with this question, strategies which may be grouped in pairs according to which of two accounts of the relationship of words to meanings they instantiate or presuppose. These accounts may be called the 'container' and the 'company' theories of meaning.

Thus, in the first place, there are those who take each word (or, at least, each substantive for, on this account, nouns are given pride of place) to contain its meaning in much the same way that bottles contain beer. Set other words alongside, and the meaning of a sentence or a paragraph builds up, rather as a wall is built of bricks. Meaning, on this account, is more or less invariant, and is only marginally affected by context or by use.

From this 'container' theory spring two opposing strategies for tackling problems of doctrinal change. There are, to begin with, those who insist that we must keep the words in order not to lose the meaning. (Of course, *new* words – from '*homoousios*' in the fourth century to 'mother' as a name for God today – are viewed with grave suspicion, because new words bring new meanings and thereby risk betrayal of the old.)

The trouble is, of course, that words do change their meaning over time. This first container strategy is doomed to failure, and those who stay attached to it, though usually called 'conservative', become, in fact, pedlars of innovation – for all the ancient terms have now acquired some new and modern meaning.

Those who adopt the second strategy, finding the old words quite unusable, and supposing the meanings they 'contain' to be the same today as they have ever been (and, therefore, as outworn as their containers), decide to change the words in order to change the meaning and thus equip themselves with words that they find 'meaningful' today. (Notice the echo of container imagery in that 'meaning*ful*'.)

This strategy works best, of course, for those, uninterested in antique notions of obedience to messages received, who suppose the standard of religious excellence to be whatever they find satisfying today and are untroubled by the fact that, very soon, a further change of fashion will demand the invention of yet another brave new creed.

Thus, through defective understanding of how words mean what they say, one group is led to lose, and the other to discard, the 'faith once for all given to the saints'.[3]

Words, in fact, take meaning from the *company* they keep. And if one, relatively stable element in meaning comes from what might be called the 'grammatical company' of cognate words with common roots (and it is this feature on which 'container' theories fasten) others come from company more literally understood both as the text or speech in which the word occurs and as each actual occasion of its use. On this account, then, it is context – actual or implied – which gives meaning to each word. (To know what 'four' means, you need first to know whether it keeps French or English company.)

Hence, a third strategy for interpreting old texts will change the words in order to secure, so far as possible, the ancient meaning. Thus, Karl Rahner used to argue for a cornucopian profusion of 'basic credal statements of the faith', which would vary not only according to national and cultural context, but also in relation to such other world-religions as formed each fresh creed's company, and to the age and education of the group for whose use it was intended (his own attempts seem mostly to have had German professors of philosophy in mind!).[4]

Rahner's proposal makes good sense, although one should not underestimate the daunting labour of interpretation necessary in order for the elements in this vast credal network to be mutually recognizable as versions of a common faith, variations on a single theme, a common story of God's relationship towards the world. Indeed, Rahner recognized that, although the Apostles' Creed can no longer 'simply perform the function of a basic summary of the faith today in an adequate way because it does not appeal directly enough to our contemporary intellectual and spiritual situation', it is still 'used in all of the Christian churches', will survive in use, and will 'always be a permanent and binding norm of faith'.[5]

It therefore seemed a good idea to adopt a fourth strategy, complementary to Karl Rahner's: namely, to leave the Apostles' Creed in place and to offer a reasonably brief and, so far as possible, non-technical reading or interpretation of its text in order to help readers who inhabit a cultural context similar to my own to make what I understand to be good sense of it, against the grain of widespread contemporary misreadings. My aim, in other words, is to provide a kind of company for the Creed in order to throw fresh light (as it may seem) upon its ancient words.

4. Why the Apostles' Creed?

To adapt a principle that I have invoked already: what the passion narratives say at length, the Creed says briefly. And, of course, some of the earliest concise expressions of Christian faith were very brief indeed: 'Jesus Christ is Lord'; 'God has made him both Lord and Christ, this Jesus whom you crucified'.[6]

It is not necessary, for my purposes, to trace what is known of the complex processes whereby, from such beginnings, the classic creeds were formed in response to the needs of baptismal preparation, doctrinal controversy and witness in times of persecution. Nevertheless, I do need to address the question: why take this creed, rather than some earlier, later, or different form of the confession of faith?

Antiquity is, of course, one consideration. Although the earliest known example of the text in almost exactly the form in which we have it dates only from an eighth century sermon of Abbot

Pirminius, the old Roman creed of which ours has been called a provincial elaboration can be traced back at least to a Roman synod in the year 340 for which bishop Marcellus of Ancyra wrote (in Greek) to Pope Julius I to protest his orthodoxy and to demonstrate that his church shared the faith of the church of Rome.[7]

What we have, then, in the Apostles' Creed, is a form already 'classical' in the fourth century which would, by the eighth, supersede all other Latin versions. It is, admittedly, a Western creed, but, especially where texts of this antiquity are concerned, it is misleading sharply to contrast 'Greek' and 'Latin' casts of mind or styles of theological imagination. This is not to say, of course, that differences should be ignored. Thus, for example, Western creeds tend simply to begin 'I believe in God', whereas the East lays more explicit emphasis upon uniqueness: 'I believe in one God ... and in one Lord Jesus Christ.' And, of course, the great councils in the East elaborated, at Nicaea, the clauses of the second article and, at Constantinople, those of the third. We shall keep an eye on these things as we go along but, for my purposes, there is much to be said for taking as my reference point the simpler and most familiar version.

Antiquity alone would not, of course, decide the matter. Indeed, the theological primitivism which supposes that the closer an idea or a practice is in time to Jesus Christ, the better it interprets him, ignores the fact that, as Newman used to say, great acts take time. It took time for Christians to begin to clarify just what it was which differentiated their faith from that of other Jewish groups. It took time for them to work out that, although Christianity remains a version or interpretation of the faith of Israel, it was nonetheless not necessary, in order to be a Christian, to be a Jew. Above all, it took time to find ways of putting the word 'God' to the quite new uses which they now discovered to be necessary if they were to do justice to what they had to say. Great acts take time, and it took Christians three hundred years before they could articulate their faith in ways which their successors, during the next one thousand six hundred years, would see no good or at least sufficient reason to discard or supersede.

This is perhaps the most surprising thing about the great fourth-century creeds: namely, that across the sea-changes of culture, circumstance and philosophy which stand between the later Roman Empire and the twilight of the modern world; across the widening gulf of mutual incomprehension separating Eastern and Western Christianity and the bitter disputes of the Reformation; notwithstanding the pressure generated by the attempt (however tragically distorted by ethnocentric insensitivity and imperial arrogance) to preach the gospel in new worlds from China to Africa, from the Argentine to India; the authority and status of the Apostles' and the Nicene Creeds should stand almost unimpaired.

Unimpaired, one should perhaps say, until recently. Renewed confusion between tradition and control (a confusion so typical of the Enlightenment but now, surprisingly, quite often found in people who suppose themselves 'postmodern') renders suspect all symbols of authoritative utterance. If the requirements of cultural pluralism, and the concerns of feminist and liberation theologies, are properly to be met, we therefore need seriously to debate the choice between superseding and interpreting the ancient creeds. But, on this issue, I have already indicated where I stand.

Although the Apostles' Creed found its final form (if we discount minor and temporary deviations, such as Luther's substitution of 'Christian' for 'Catholic' in the Small Catechism of 1529) well over a millennium ago, the history of the Creed continued, not only in the sense that, at one level, the history of Christianity simply *is* the history of the interpretation of Scripture and of Creed, but also in the sense that fresh crises continued to generate fresh confessions – most of which incorporated and none of which were intended to replace the classic creeds.[8]

Many of these confessions (that of Augsburg, for example) were of considerable length. Some, on the Catholic side, beginning with that promulgated by Pope Paul IV in 1564, consist of the creeds of Nicaea and Constantinople to which are appended other propositions. (All this notwithstanding the fact that the Council of Chalcedon had forbidden the composition of any further creeds!) And Newman, it willl be remembered, found in his principle of 'development' of doctrine the answer to the charge which he himself had levelled against the Catholic Church: namely, that it had departed from the truth by 'adding' items to the Creed.

It seems of first importance, therefore, to continue to insist that no 'additions' to the Creed are possible, for reasons which will bring us back to where we started: namely, to consideration of how things hang together.[9]

If the Creed were a catalogue or list of things believed, there would then seem, in principle, to be no reason why that list should not be extended. As the practice of constitutional amendment indicates, a group of people may well wish, from time to time, to modify – by addition, deletion or amendment – whatever charter or other instrument encodes its declaration of identity and purpose.

Credal confession is, indeed, the declaration of identity-sustaining rules of discourse and behaviour governing Christian uses of the word 'God'. There are, therefore, evidently some affinities between its function and that of such constitutional instruments. Moreover, as we have already seen, credal declaration has, from the beginning, found expression in more succinct and more elaborate forms – and, in order to elaborate, one *adds* more words!

Nevertheless, bearing the narrative character of the Creed in mind, we need to notice that the difference between telling a story briefly and telling the same story in more detail, and at greater length, is not always best described by saying that we have 'added' something to the tale. Indeed, even in matters as mundane as giving evidence in court, there may well be statements the use of which is such as to make the distinction between 'addition' and 'elaboration' a far weightier matter than any mere consideration of academic pedantry.

The Creed is such a case. There may be many things which, as Christians, we believe, but we seriously misunderstand the grammar of the Creed if we suppose its primary purpose to be that of furnishing a list of them. To say the Creed is to say, not many things, but one. To say the Creed is to perform an act which has one object: right worship of the mystery of God. To say the Creed is to confess, beyond all conflict and confusion, our trust in One who makes and heals the world and who makes all things one. It is not possible to make additions to the Creed because, in using it, we have but one thing to say in recognition, praise and wonder: 'Yes', 'Amen'. And as to why this one thing should be three ways said: that is the subject-matter of this book.

them in the Creed, these words did not mean what we usually mean by 'believe'. The point is not that the Creed was mistranslated but that, since the English word 'believe' was born, it has profoundly changed its meaning. Like *credo* and *pisteuo*, in their Christian uses, it was originally what we call a 'performative': one of those words which, instead of describing or evaluating some state of affairs, enacts what it announces, like 'I promise' or 'I pledge'.[3]

Thus, as we use it in the Creed, in a public act of worship, 'I believe' does not express an opinion, however well founded or firmly held, concerning God's existence. It promises that life and love, mind, heart, and all my actions, are set henceforward steadfastly on God, and God alone. 'William James, do you take Mary Montague to be your lawful wedded wife?' 'I do'. 'Mary Montague, do you believe in God the Father almighty, creator of heaven and earth?' 'I do.' The grammar of these two declarations is the same.

In credal confession, as in the exchange of marriage vows, the making of such weighty promises entails or presupposes a vast and varied range of opinions held and people trusted, entails (in other words) a complex of 'beliefs'. Moreover, responsibly to make such promises requires that the beliefs which they entail be tried and tested. Christian faith is no more arbitrary, speculative or irrational than is its particular expression in Christian marriage. (It would be most imprudent to enter into matrimony with someone concerning whose reliability or even whose existence one harboured the gravest doubts!) Nevertheless, making a promise is one thing, and announcing the grounds on which we make it is another. In its primary use, as public confession of faith, 'I believe in God' does not state an opinion or express an attitude; it makes a promise.

Promises, freely entered into, may be withheld. Should we then say that we 'choose' to believe? Not if such language leads us to forget that it is first a question of our being chosen. So, to rephrase it: is the response of faith appropriately described as a matter of choice, or decision, on our part? Much depends upon the way in which such choices are presented to the imagination. All talk of 'wagers' or of 'leaps of faith', for instance, is best avoided. Commitment does entail conviction, and deep convictions are not hazarded but grown into; slowly, obscurely and often painfully acquired. They are the fruit of experience, not the outcome of some more or less arbitrary effort of the will. Apparent or occasional exceptions set aside, it make no more sense to suppose that someone could move, overnight, from a religious 'nowhere' (as it were) into the kind of life-long self-bestowal which finds expression in the Creed, than that they could 'jump' into comparably complex social or political commitments. Great acts take time.

Perhaps the least misleading way to characterize the element of decision in confession of faith would be to say that we acknowledge it to be risk-laden. There is an element of risk in all exercises of personal responsibility. We cannot endlessly keep all our options open in respect of everything and everybody. The alternative to risk and venture, in human existence, is not rationality and prudence, but the irresponsible dilettantism which we call 'bad faith'.

Moreover, by drawing attention to the vulnerability of faith, to the risk-laden character of the promises we make, we are brought back to that constitutive tension which I mentioned in the previous chapter, between commitment and enquiry, declaration and investigation, short words and endless learning. Few Christian thinkers, in modern times, have laid more strenuous emphasis than Newman did on the attainability of certitude in matters of belief. But Newman also knew that such certitude was only appropriately won, endured, tested and sustained, in full exposure to the hazards and uncertainties of our existence. That is why, throughout his life, he insisted that the life of faith, the enactment of the promise that is made in baptism and renewed whenever we recite the Creed, is best spoken of in terms of 'risk' and 'venture'. To a correspondent who objected to his speaking of '*venturing* in matters of faith', Newman replied: 'Did not Abraham, my dear Sir, make a venture, when he went out, not knowing whither he went?'[4]

2. Believing in God

And now, perhaps, we can at last move on to speak of God. Not quite. There is one more ambush laid across our path: the seemingly innocent word 'in'. 'I do not believe in taking pills'; 'Do you believe in ghosts?' – the construction is so familiar in English that, at first sight, it is hard to see why all the commentators, from Augustine onwards, should have been so preoccupied with the strange notion that, as Christians, we believe 'in' God. Augustine's distinction between three Latin constructions – '*credere Deo*', '*credere Deum*' and '*credere in Deum*' – exercised a massive influence on later Christian thought. I shall accordingly take his account, and Aquinas's interpretation of it, as my guide.

'*Credere Deo*', according to Augustine, is a matter of believing what God says or, as we would say, 'believing God'. '*Credere Deum*' is a matter of believing God to be God. Unfortunately, the most natural English rendering of this would be 'believing in God' – taking this phrase to cover either one or both of: acknowledging that God exists and supposing that the 'God' we speak of is, we might say, the only real God. In any of these senses of 'belief', Augustine adds laconically, demons and evildoers may believe in God. It follows that '*Credo in Deum*', as it stands at the head of the Apostles' Creed, does not mean any of the things that we might most naturally take 'I believe in God' to mean.

Faith, for Aquinas as for Augustine, is the way in which, in this life, we know God. (We may have some difficulty with this idea because, in modern English usage, we tend – on the basis of distinctions sharply drawn between 'merely believing' things and knowing them – to keep faith and knowledge quite some way apart.) Aquinas takes up Augustine's distinction, and suggests that God may be understood to be, in three ways, the 'object' of our faith. First, in the sense of what faith knows or has in mind; this is what it is '*credere Deum*', to believe in God. Second, in the sense of the point of view from which faith knows whatever it knows (including God); this is what it is '*credere Deo*', to believe God. Under this second head, in other words, faith is considered as our response to what God says, to God's uttered Word.

And the third sense? This is Augustine's '*credere in Deum*', under which heading God is the object of our faith as heart's desire, as goal towards which all our life and thought is set, as (we might almost say) faith's 'objective'. One translator tries 'believing unto God', but this is an awkward and unfamiliar expression. Augustine says it better: 'What is it, therefore, to believe in him [*credere in eum*]? It is in believing to love, in believing to delight, in believing to walk towards him, and be incorporated amongst the limbs or members of his body.'[5]

Thus, our consideration of that small word 'in' brings us to the same point that we reached in the previous chapter. To confess belief in God is to set all our life, our mind, our heart, in God's direction.

But which direction might that be? Not, we must begin by saying, the direction of any goal, ideal, ambition, dream, fulfilment, peace, or beauty we can think of. If we are to speak some sense of God, to say something appropriate, we can only do so under the controlling rubric that whatever can be depicted in words or images, stories or ideas, is not God. We do not know what 'God' means.

Why, then, continue to use the word at all? Most people, these days, seem to get on quite well without it! This is an issue to which we shall return. For the time being, it is sufficient to insist that 'believing in God' is not a matter of believing in any particular fact, thing, object, person, idea, or state of affairs, because all these are categories of items that constitute the world – categories, in other words, of creatures.

The point needs to be more strongly made: believing in God entails *not* 'believing in' (in the sense of that phrase that we have indicated) anything else. We educated Westerners are, for the most part, so little tempted by beliefs and practices which we would *deem* to be idolatrous that we find it hard to notice the firmness of the grip in which we are held by the dominant idolatries of our culture. Idolatry is worship of creatures, of particular things. It is, therefore, in the terminology of the Creed, a matter of 'believing in' creatures, and all human beings have their hearts set *somewhere* – if only on themselves. For most of us, there is probably no single creature that is the object of our faith. Most of us, in other words, are polytheists. And none of us is so self-transparent as to know quite where it is, in fact, our hearts are set. None of us knows for sure what is the 'object' of our faith, what it is that we 'believe in'.

Against this background, Christianity is perhaps best seen as an *educative* project: as providing a context in which human beings may learn, however slowly, partially, imperfectly, some freedom from the destructive bondage which the worship of any creature – however large or powerful, beautiful or terrifying, interesting or important – brings.

Being thus weaned from our idolatry is not, however, a question of 'detachment', if by this we mean coming to suppose that nothing really matters. On the contrary, it is a question of being brought, like blind people towards eyesight, into some clearer, more accurate and honest understanding of the way things are and might be made to be. If faith is the way in which, in this life, we know God, then learning to 'believe in' God is learning to see all things in the way God sees them: as worth infinite expenditure of understanding, interest, and care.

The form and context of faith's movement towards its unseen goal in God is, therefore, the never-finished eminently practical affair of working to establish, between creatures, appropriate relationships of justice, reconciliation and compassion (this, after all, was the message of Israel's prophets). 'Believing in God', in other words, far from being the kind of affair for the private heart which so many in our culture take to be the business of 'religion' or 'spirituality', requires comprehensive interest and engagement in questions of culture, politics, and ecology. 'Believing in God', far from taking us *away* from the world God makes, opens up, ineluctably, to the demands of justice, peace, and the integrity of all creation.

3. Believing in one God

The Nicene Creed spells out what the Apostles' Creed assumes: that we believe in 'one' God. Just as we found to be the case with both 'believe' and 'in', we have here yet another straightforward and familiar word which it is very difficult to use properly of God. There are (as the discerning reader will by now have noticed) two reasons why this is so. In the first place, we are dealing with an ancient text, a text whose versions and translations have been put to use, interpreted and argued over, in a wide range of different cultural, political and intellectual circumstances. The Creed has a long history.

In the second place, learning to use the Creed is one small part of the lifelong enterprise of learning that there is nothing that may easily be said of God; that, if we find it easy to say certain things of God, the chances are that, when we say them, we lose sight of God. Learning to watch our language when we say the Creed is just one aspect of our education into courtesy towards God's creatures and silence before the mystery of God.

The oneness or identity of something is (I suggested in the previous chapter) the way it hangs together, is made one, is brought under some appropriate description or into some single story. But none of this is what we mean when we say God is 'one'.

In the first place, there is no way that God is 'made' one, nor does God 'hang together'. Such expressions apply only to things with bits or parts or episodes. But absolutely everyone and everything that we have ever known, imagined, thought about or undergone is thus 'made'. We therefore have no way, in language or imagination, of handling anything that is not 'made'. When we say that *God* is 'one', we mean, not that God 'hangs together' but that he does not, for God has neither episodes or parts. To say this, or attempt to do so, is thus to put that small word 'one' to strange new uses which we can neither handle nor control.

It follows, in the second place, that to confess God as 'one' is to acknowledge the impossibility of bringing him under some appropriate description or into some single story we could tell. Hence the emphasis, characteristic of Christianity but by no means confined to it, on what is known as 'negative theology': the disciplined insistence on 'unknowing', the acknowledgment that even the things we find ourselves enabled or allowed or required to say of God are said in 'fear and trembling', in recognition that what we say is quite beyond us. God's oneness is beyond our comprehension.

By now, some irritated reader may be muttering: but surely there is at least one quite straightforward implication of our confession of faith in *one* God; namely the rejection of all *other* gods as idols, as false gods, as unreal? This is true, in the sense that Christianity, like Judaism and Islam, has always resisted the division of our hearts, insisting that there is but one proper object of our hopes, desires and dreams, our loyalty, promises and trust.

'I believe in one God' does, therefore, as used by Christians, entail the belief that there is only one God. But even this apparently innocent expression can be dangerous. A few years ago, the Seychelles warbler was on the edge of extinction: only some twenty individuals survived. Happily, this story ended well, and the species now flourishes and is protected on the tiny island of Cousin. But it was a close shave: we nearly reached the situation in which some naturalist might sensibly have said 'I believe that there is only one Seychelles warbler'. Other naturalists might (equally sensibly) have disagreed, contending that there were still several specimens, or none, or, indeed, that the species had been, from the start, a classificatory error, a figment of the scientific imagination.

I apologize for this pedestrian parable, but some people seem to think that 'I believe in one God' means something like: 'I believe that the species *deus* has one and only one instantiation'. But God is not a member of a species, an individual with a nature. (If he were, that would be how he hung together, how God was the kind of creature that he was!) Some people, accordingly, suggest that we insist that God is not a god. This may be true, but does not seem particularly helpful. Others have suggested that the word 'God' is now so burdened with misunderstanding and misuse that we would do better to discard it. Perhaps, but on the whole it seems more likely that the surrender of the term would contribute to our forgetfulness of God, would reinforce our propensity for egotism, short-sightedness and despair, than that it would help keep us watchful and attentive to the presence of the healing mystery that makes us and all things one.

'I believe in one God.' Perhaps the aspect of this confession which least requires the discipline of continual negation (and which also, incidentally, brings out how very *Jewish* Christian faith remains) is its expression of our trust in the reliability, integrity, unswerving loyalty of God. God is not capricious, wayward, as we are – whose fragile oneness is made from most unstable and often warring elements. Much modern criticism of the doctrine of God's 'immutability' fails to appreciate that, at its heart, this doctrine speaks of and celebrates the faithfulness of One who does not change his mind. (Forgiveness, as we shall see, is not God's change of his mind, but of ours.)

I said earlier that God is not an individual with a nature. Natures are kinds and categories, and the One we worship is beyond all categories, creates and comprehends all kinds. For most of Christian history, it was neo-Platonism which provided the richest symbolic and conceptual resources for giving expression to this recognition and to the disciplined negation it requires. It would, however, be quite wrong to suppose that it could not find expression in other and very different forms. Thus, for example, not only is it what we might call an emergent property of Jewish faith, but the more that 'Westerners' learn of Hinduism, Buddhism and Islam, the more likely it seems that, in due time, Christians will be able to give quite fresh expression to what will still be, recognizably, a common faith in the singleness, and 'simpleness', and faithfulness, of God.

If God were an individual with a nature we could, in principle, presumably, give some direct account of what that nature was. But, since God is not a creature, an object of some kind, what we continue (nevertheless!) to call God's 'nature' can only be spoken of indirectly, under the discipline of negation, and in abstraction from the modes or aspects of our relationship to him.

But, if this strange, much-battered, elusive and more or less unintelligible word 'God' is so difficult to use, why not go straight to the point and speak – as I shall do, following the contours of the Creed, through the remaining chapters of this book – of the mystery we know as Father, Son, and Spirit? The short answer to this question is that, should someone ask: 'But are not these three one?', they would be told they were; and should the questioner then ask: 'One *what*?', this question would, in turn, deserve an answer. I have so far done no more in this chapter than indicate some of the elements of such an answer.

'I believe in one God.' In confessing our Christian faith through recitation of the Creed, we are issuing a single declaration, pledging ourselves to work towards that comprehensive healing, one-making or at-one-ment, of us and all the world, by which all things are brought to share the unimaginable singleness or harmony which is God's alone.

4. How many articles?

God may not be made or hang together, but the Creed in which we confess our faith in God undoubtedly both is and does. It hangs together, not as a heap or catalogue, but as a structured whole, the elements of which are hinged, 'articulated'. How many articles, then, does the Apostles' Creed contain?

The answer that I remember learning, as a child, was 'twelve'. There was a legend, already widespread by the fifth century, which traced this view back to the Spirit's descent at Pentecost, inspiring each of the twelve apostles in turn: Peter said, 'I believe in God, the Father almighty ...'; Andrew added, 'And in Jesus Christ, his only Son, our Lord', and so on round the table (the allocation of clauses to apostles varying in the different versions). As Ambrose succinctly put it: 'Just as there are twelve apostles, so too there are twelve expressions [*sententiae*].'[6]

As a teaching aid and reminder of our apostolic origins, this charming story may do no great harm. Much depends upon the religious and intellectual climate of its use. Thus, in the measure that the items making up the Creed came to be treated as primarily a list of different things to be believed, the idea that there were twelve articles obscured from view the actual structure of the Creed and, by so doing, risked distorting the character of Christian faith, whose direct object is not some set of propositions, however correct and indispensable, but the single mystery, eliciting our whole heart's response, in whom all truth is integrated and made one.

This one confession finds expression in three articles. Historically, there is no doubt whatsoever but that the Creed, like the baptismal formulas from which it derived, is trinitarian in form. It has three articles, confessing faith in Father, Son, and Spirit. And those same teachers who, in the early centuries, used the story of the twelve-fold inspiration of the twelve apostles, were resolute in their insistence on the Creed's reflection of the threefold structure of the single mystery of faith. But, if this is so, what are the warrants for my apparent *fourfold* distribution of the elements of the Creed? Surely, this chapter should have been subtitled 'I believe in', and the next: 'God, the Father almighty, creator of heaven and earth'?

In order to answer this question, we need to go right back to the Jewish origins of Christian faith. The history of Israel's names for God is complex and obscure. There are, however, three features of it which may be isolated for our purposes. In the first place, common or descriptive names were used, betokening power and strength; names evoking reverence and awe; names such as *El* and *Elohim*. Unable as we are to take quite seriously what we think of as 'divinities' or 'gods' (hence the patronizing tone of so much anthropology and ancient history), we find these terms difficult to translate without dilution. In the second place, the history of these common names came to be interwoven with that of the term which, in due course, acquired the status of the proper name of Israel's god: the term 'Yahweh'. It is still uncertain quite what this term means. It is possibly best taken as simultaneously a disclosure of God's reliability and a refusal to provide the people with a 'name' – a 'handle', we might say – with which they could pin down the mystery that summoned them, as it had led their fathers, into that unknown future in which the promises would find fulfilment. In the third place, post-exilic Judaism tended, out of reverence, to replace all 'names' of God with honorifics and, especially, with 'Lord' (the Hebrew *Adonai* and Greek *Kurios*).

There was in Greek, of course, another word to hand, a word used by the Greek translators of the Hebrew Scriptures to translate *El* and *Elohim*: the word *theos*. Outside Judaism and Christianity, the '*theoi*' were the powers of order, form and meaning; powers penetrating the whole world with their influence, restoring chaos to coherence. Now, this word *theos* is put to quite new use, its fundamental frame of reference shifted (to put it crudely) from cosmos to history, as it is applied first to Israel's Lord and, later, to him now confessed as Father of our Lord Jesus Christ.

Thus, as Karl Rahner demonstrated in an influential article, in the New Testament *ho theos* (with the definite article) refers to God the Father, and it is equally certain that, in the baptismal and early versions of the Creed, it is as 'Father' that God is confessed.[7] So far, then, we have found nothing to warrant my arrangement.

The moral of the story, for Rahner, was that the so-called 'Greek' view of God's Trinity is closer to biblical usage than that called 'Latin'. The latter proceeds from the oneness of God's nature to consideration of the persons; the former begins with the Father, 'wellspring of divinity', source from which both Son and Spirit proceed. Thus, in the Greek view, 'the unity and integrity of the divine nature is conceptually a *consequence* of the fact that the Father communicates his whole nature'.[8] It is, in other words, only *as* Source, and Son, and Spirit, that God is known. But, in thus knowing them, it is one God that is known.

Already, within the New Testament, the expression *ho theos*, which originally only signified the Father, was 'slowly, as it were shyly and cautiously ... detached from him', and also used of Christ and, later, of the Spirit.[9] The new things which Christians wished to say could not be easily or quickly said. Great acts take time. It took four hundred years before what was eventually deemed satisfactory expression could be found for the conviction that, without jeopardy to the singleness of simpleness of God, God's *whole* self is given in begotten Son and breathed in outpoured Spirit.

Already, by Augustine's time, the axiom that whatever God does that is not God is done, indivisibly, by all three persons, was firmly established in Latin thought: 'just as Father and Son and Holy Spirit are inseparable, so do they work inseparably'.[10] In itself, the principle enunciated here is indispensable, for God simply is God's deed, and act, and utterance. Unfortunately, the way in which the principle was handled, in much Western theology, led in due course to the dissociation of consideration of God's creative and redemptive work from consideration of the doctrine of God's Trinity – thereby relegating the very heart and centre of the Christian faith to the margins of most people's piety, thought and practice.

In reaction, there is now a fashion in some Western theology to say that the Latins simply got it wrong and that only the Greek view can properly safeguard the Christian sense of God inherited from Scripture and tradition. We would, in my opinion, be better advised to try sufficiently to deepen and enrich our understanding of *both* approaches as to enable us to draw upon their distinctive strengths without succumbing to their weaknesses.

The strength of the Greek view is, undoubtedly, the close bond it secures between the way in which the mystery of God is known to us and the framework within which we seek to give that mystery unified and coherent intellectual expression. The weakness, however, is that in a culture such as ours which no longer shares the narratives and symbol systems in which that framework was first forged, we are in danger of being left with only the most notional and fragile imaginative purchase upon the *unity* of God.

Rahner is, I think, correct to say that, on the Greek view, 'the unity and integrity of the divine nature is conceptually a consequence of the fact that the Father communicates his whole nature'.[11] The key word there, however, is 'conceptually'. That God is one, with radical and absolute integrity and simpleness entirely beyond our understanding and imagination, formed the very atmosphere which the Greek Fathers breathed. Their *understanding* of this given truth was drawn out and derived from consideration of the completeness of God's self-communication. But what was for them context and presupposition is not so for us. For us, a view of the doctrine of God's Trinity which treats the unity of God, intellectually, as 'consequence', is likely, in practice, to set the question of that unity to one side as not of burning interest, a merely academic or theoretical affair (thus leading the admirers of the Greek view into the mirror-image of that trap into which they suppose the Latins to have fallen!).

If we, inhabitants of modern Western culture, would faithfully interpret not only the Latins but the Greeks as well, we need to keep the question of God's oneness centre stage. It should be possible to do this, while yet avoiding the one-sidedness into which the Latins fell, if we insist that all we know of God is known, and only known, in and through our relationships with Father, Son and Spirit. Thus, for example (to anticipate matters which we shall consider in the next chapter), from the fact that 'Father and Son and Holy Spirit . . . work inseparably' in creation; the fact – in other words – that the answer to the question 'Who creates the world?' is 'God', it need not and, indeed, should not be inferred that there is not more to be said concerning the distinct relationships which we enjoy, as creatures, with Father, Son and Spirit, in their one single work.

To return, at length, to the question from which I set out. My distribution of the elements of the Creed is not, in fact, fourfold. In the attempt to give due weight, in the circumstances of the time and place in which I write, to what seem to me the strengths of both Eastern and Western approaches to the doctrine of God's Trinity, I have (in this chapter and the one before) simply sought to preface my consideration of the three articles of the Creed with discussion of some of the questions – for the most part, formal or philosophical in character – which, in our culture, are prompted by the first four words of the Apostles' Creed. (I note with interest, incidentally, that the ICET translation of the Apostles' Creed not only introduces each of the three articles with 'I believe in' but, in the first clause, puts a comma after 'God'. For both of which, my thanks.)

5. *Believing three ways in one God*

In contemporary preaching and instruction, the most widespread presentation of the Creed is probably not as a collection of twelve articles but rather as summarizing the plot of a drama with three acts. First, God makes the world, then we make a mess of it which God sends his Son to clean up and, thirdly, God sends his Spirit to bring us back to him through faith and sacraments and holiness.

Although this scheme has much more to commend it than the notion of a catalogue of twelve beliefs, it suffers from some serious disadvantages. By treating the articles of the Creed as descriptive of three acts, three different operations done in sequence, it gives the impression that creation was what once happened in some immeasurably distant past, 'in the beginning'; that forgiveness, resurrection and life everlasting lie in some distant future, and that, in the meantime, in place of the Spirit we have the Catholic church!

In other words, what the three-act scheme obscures is that our threefold confession in the Creed declares our *present* relationship with God: with God creator, God once born and crucified, now risen, God our present life and future peace. In our uses of the Creed, we confess that we believe three ways in one God.

God is not an individual with a nature. But neither is God an agent acting in three episodes. In so far as the scheme of one drama with three acts is allowed to shape the sense of our relationship to Father, Son, and Spirit, it draws us back towards some version of the oldest of all families of trinitarian heresy, known as 'modalism'. Modalism came in many shapes and sizes, but common to them all was the conviction that, in the Godhead, the only differentiations are transitory, episodic, a matter of successive ways (or 'modes') of acting or existing. Beneath the play of light and colour, before and after the episode of incarnation, the rock of God endures, unalterable and unmoved. For the modalist, in other words, the three ways we know God are of the nature of appearances, transitory forms, 'beneath' which the divine nature, unaffected, stands.

God is not an individual with a nature, nor is God an agent acting in three episodes. According to what was, in due time, established as Christian orthodoxy, the distinctions that we draw in our attempts to speak of God go, as it were, to the very heart of the matter. The distinctions between Father, Son and Spirit are distinctions truly drawn of *God,* and not merely of the way that God appears to us to be, or of the way that – for some brief span of time – he was. We shall, in later chapters, have ample opportunity to consider what we do and do not mean when we call God 'Father', 'Son' and 'Spirit'. For the time being, my concern is simply to insist that there is no 'more' to say of God, no further story to be told, 'beyond' what such words mean.

There are three ways that we believe in God, ways which find expression in the three articles of the Creed. To be more exact: there are three ways in God, three ways God is, for each of which the term we use, conventionally, is 'person'. There are, we say, three persons in one God. Many Christians, I suspect, take this to mean that God is in some way three people. Which God, of course, is not.

There is no doubt whatsoever, to my mind, but that the arguments for ceasing to speak of 'persons' in trinitarian theology greatly outweigh those in favour of the term's retention. Let us take our bearings, once more, from Augustine. 'Because the Father is not the Son and the Son is not the Father, and the Holy Spirit who is also called the gift of God is neither the Father nor the Son, they are certainly three . . Yet when you ask "Three what?", human speech labours under a great dearth of words. So we say three persons, not in order to say that precisely, but in order not to be reduced to silence.'[12]

God, for Augustine, following the tradition in Latin theology initiated by Tertullian, is said to be one 'substance' (*substantia*) in three 'persons' (*personae*). Augustine was not impressed by the fact that Greek theologians laboured to draw distinctions between the meanings of the cognate Greek terms '*ousia*' and '*hypostasis*'; he found these attempts 'obscure'. For him, the distinction between 'substance' and 'person' in Latin terminology is 'purely and simply one of linguistic convention'.[13]

Whatever qualifications one might want to make in point of detail, this view of the matter is, I believe, in general quite correct. We call God 'one'. We call God 'three'. One what? Three whats? We might, in either case, say simply 'thing' or 'things' (for this is, after all, what the ancient terms amounted to). This would, admittedly, be inelegant but, if we insist on having an answer to the question 'three whats?', then there is something to be said for choosing an expression which does not misleadingly appear (as 'person' does) to be informative.

This, I think, is the heart of the matter. As Newman put it, we knew 'before we began to use [the term "person"], that the Son was God yet was not the Father ... the word Person tells us nothing in addition to this'.[14] In other words, to say that 'God is three persons in one nature' tells us no more about God than would 'God is three things in one thing', or than does 'God is three and God is one'.

Not only does the concept of 'person' misleadingly give the impression of telling us something about God which we would not otherwise have known, but the information that it seems to give is false. For us, a person is an individual agent, a conscious centre of memory and choice, of action, reflection and decision. But when we say there are, in God, 'three persons', we do not mean that God has, as it were, three minds, three memories, three wills.

Although the individualism which, in Western culture, infects our sense of what it is to be a human person is no help here, to exorcize it would not render the term more suitable for use in trinitarian theology. Even if we brought off the massive cultural, economic and political transformation necessary in order to set at centre stage relationship and mutuality, rather than ownership and independence, it would still be true that human beings would exist as individual agents. Amongst us, three persons would still be three people.

To put the point as succinctly as possible (because it will, I hope, be amply and less abstractly illustrated in due course): we *have* relationships, God *is* the relations that he has. I am someone who is a father. In God, fathering is what God, whom we call Father, is. Human beings do many things, including speak. And, sometimes, a good word is spoken, something worthwhile is said or done. In God, being uttered, conceived, enacted, understood, is what God, whom we call Word or *Logos*, is. And so on. God, we might say, is relationship without remainder, which we, most certainly, are not.

Credal confession, I said earlier, is the declaration of identity-sustaining rules of discourse and behaviour governing Christian uses of the word 'God'. We learn to use this word well, not by attempting to gain some purchase on God's 'nature', but by learning to live, and think, and work, and suffer, within the pattern of trinitarian relations which the Creed supplies.

God is not an individual with a nature; nor is God an agent acting in three episodes; nor is God three people. The three articles of the Apostles' Creed, articles which speak, in turn, of Father, Son and Spirit, do not each deal with one *part* of Christian doctrine – for Father, Son, and Spirit are not 'parts' of God. Each article speaks of the single mystery that we call God and, therefore, each of them says something of the *whole* of Christian faith, of how all things hang together in relation to God's holy mystery. There are three articles because there are, in God, three ways, three 'modes of being'.

To consider any one of these in isolation or abstraction from the other two would compromise our recognition of the singleness or simpleness of God. It follows, therefore, that nothing that is said of any one of them will be appropriately said except in relation to the other two. At every turn, our understanding of one 'person' will be modified, adjusted, and corrected from the standpoint of our understanding of the others. This is what I had in mind when I said earlier that the very form of the Creed provides a pattern of self-correction, of restraint upon the range of its misuse. And this is also why, in each of the next three chapters, I shall follow the discussion of whichever aspect of the mystery forms the 'focus' of that particular article with some remarks on the relationship between that article and other two. My hope is in this way to display somewhat more thoroughly than do many of the commentaries the radically trinitarian character of human existence lived and understood within the framework furnished by the Creed.

IV

Producing

'The Father almighty, creator of heaven and earth.'

In the earliest confessions of Christian faith, it was the fatherhood of God which formed the focus of this first article; a fatherhood of one acknowledged to be 'all-ruling'. (My gratitude to ICET was, at least in part, premature. If one wished to capture the emphases of the early centuries, 'God the Father, almighty', would probably be a better punctuation than 'God, the Father almighty'.)

Although, in the East, God was, from the beginning, confessed as 'maker' of the world, it would be several centuries before 'creator of heaven and earth' settled into the Western creeds, and then only after a period of hesitation as to whether 'founder', 'establisher' (translations of *conditor*) or 'creator' was to be preferred (the choice of the latter perhaps being influenced by the fact that this was the word found, in the Latin Vulgate, at the opening of the Book of Genesis).

Father of what, or whom, is God confessed to be? Second-century Christians would, for the most part, have answered: of all of us and all the world. Thus Tatian, writing only some sixty or seventy years after the completion of the Fourth Gospel, speaks of God as 'Father of things tangible and things unseen'.[1] Christological controversy would, in due course, narrow the focus, concentrating attention on God's fatherhood of Jesus Christ, his only Son.

'Almighty' translates *omnipotens*, omnipotent, suggesting a capacity to do whatever one wants. But, behind them both, the Greek word *pantocrator* had, in the Christian usage of the first three centuries as in the Greek translation of the Old Testament, the more active sense of exercise of sovereign power.[2]

For most Christians these days, it is probably the word 'creator' which forms the imaginative focus of the first article of the Apostles' Creed. This, at least, I have assumed in taking the doctrine of creation as the central theme of this chapter. What the Scriptures say at length, the Creed says briefly. I hope that these remarks on terminology may already at least have hinted at the centrality, for Jewish and early Christian versions of what we would call doctrines of creation, of the image of beneficent and effective kingship. Quite what so apparently alien and, for many people, so alienating an image has still to offer, we shall consider in due course.

Finally, my aim in taking active, verbal forms – producing, appearing, peacemaking – as key words for the articles of the Creed is to help keep the entire discussion within the framework of the establishment, the fostering, the fracturing, of relationships: of relations between human beings, between human beings and other creatures, between all creatures and the mystery of God; and, beyond all this and at the heart of it, of that trinitarian pattern of relations between Father, Son and Spirit – or, we might say, at least provisionally, between Producer, Appearance and Peace – which the unknown God is, in the Creed, confessed to be.

1. Creating

Who creates the world? This does not seem to be a question which should cause much difficulty because the answer, obviously, is God. But some people these days, troubled (for example) by the apparent gender-tone onesideness of 'Father', prefer not to speak of God as Father, Son and Spirit, but rather as Creator, Redeemer and Sanctifier, thus taking the term 'Creator' to refer, more narrowly, to only one of the three whom God is said to be.

There are two issues here: a particular issue concerning the identity of the creator, and a more general question as to how we might best decide which words to use of God, without further specification of their reference, and which to use of only one of God's three modes or aspects.

As to the general issue, I know of no good reason why we should modify or call in question the long-established principle that the persons in God are only to be distinguished from each other in terms of the 'relationships of origin' which they are said to be. Thus (to take the easiest example) only the Father is to be called Father, and only the Son called Son. Neither 'creator' nor 'almighty', however, are terms descriptive of such relationships. It is, therefore, simply to God and not primarily (let alone exclusively) to Father, Son, or Spirit, that being 'creator' or 'almighty' is to be ascribed.

This last statement, though correct, does call for clarification if it is not to be misunderstood. I earlier endorsed the principle that whatever God does that is not God is done, indivisibly, by all three persons. From which it follows that it is by all three, as one single work, that the world is made.

But indivisibly does not mean indifferently. God does one work, which is the world, but does that one work differently. One standard way of putting this would be to say that God, the Father, creates through the Son in the Spirit. God is like an artist who does her work by having an idea and lovingly effecting it. She creates, that is to say, through uttered Word and given Love.[3]

At least at first sight, such expressions do, however, seem fatally to trade upon an ambiguity. Surely the agent, in such stories, is not all three persons acting indivisibly but only the one that we call 'father'? At which point we need to bear in mind, not only that the doctrine of God's Trinity has a history but that, even in what might be called its fully-fashioned form, it has an order, shape or pattern. The pattern, moreover, grew out of the history. Even when the point is reached at which it is most strenuously insisted that God is, equally, all three – that the Spirit, and the Son, are no 'less' God than is the Father – even then, the Father still remains, as 'Father' or progenitor, the source or principle, the 'Godhead's spring' or *fons divinitatis*, in the one still movement that is the life of God. (I shall attempt in the next section to address the feminist concerns which arise, quite legitimately as it seems to me, at this point.) As a result, the very dynamic of the metaphors, the movement they describe, suggests that – while standing firm by the contention that the proper answer to the question 'Who creates the world?' is 'God' – there still remain good reasons for speaking especially of God, the Father, as creator or producer of the world. (And St Thomas, who shows great good sense in these matters, acknowledges this in the passage to which I earlier referred.)

The easy way to read all this would be (to mention one more ancient heresy) 'subordinationist'; would be to settle, in other words, for taking almost literally the metaphor of the artist, thereby reducing Word and Spirit to actions of the Father who, alone, would *really* count as God. But this would be to set at naught the effort and the energy expended, over several centuries, as Christians strove to bend such metaphors to much more interesting use.

At the heart of classical trinitarian theology is the conviction that the one who remains the unknown God is, nevertheless, wholly expressed in uttered Word and given in outpoured Love; that God, we might say, puts himself entirely into the life he is and work he does. Suppose, then, that instead of lazily assuming that the doctrine more or less boils down to saying the very thing that those who forged it struggled not to say, we turn the tables round and entertain the possibility that growth in understanding of the unknown God is to a large extent a matter of learning to put more of ourselves into everything we are and do, thereby becoming a little more alive and thus participating somewhat better in God's creative work?

If God does one work, which is the world, when is that work done? This question is answered at the beginning of the Bible, in the first verse of the Book of Genesis (or 'beginnings'): 'In the beginning God created the heavens and the earth.'[4] The people of Israel were not, of course, unique in having a cosmogony, a story of how the world, or cosmos, came to be. All people tell such stories. However, in order to compare the different versions different people tell, it is important to ascertain, in each particular case, the purpose, scope and function of the narrative.

Thus, for example, natural scientists are very interested, these days, in the beginning of the world. And the sales of Stephen Hawking's *A Brief History of Time* bear witness to widespread fascination with what the scientist has to say about creation.[5] Moreover, those scientists who are also interested in theology take it for granted that such information as they and their colleagues have acquired about the world's beginning supplies the standard against which to test the statement 'In the beginning God created the heavens and the earth.' But this assumption rests upon two more, both of which, in fact, are false. It is assumed, first, that Christian doctrines of creation make claims about the initial conditions of the world, and, secondly, that in these doctrines the concept of God serves as a principle of explanation. Some episodes in the recent history of the discussion may help to make the issues clear.

According to a former Scottish Astronomer Royal, 'When we speak of the "beginning" of the Universe, we always mean the time to which we can trace back ultimately all the various phenomena which we now observe.' Until quite recently, that beginning, the moment of the Big Bang, was imagined as a kind of point, a pinprick concentration of unimaginable intensity, from which all else proceeds. But does that moment have, shall we say, a *context* and, if so, what might be said of it? According to another most distinguished scientist, Sir Edmund Whittaker (in 1942): 'When by purely scientific methods we trace the development of the material Universe backwards in time, we arrive ultimately at a critical state of affairs beyond which the laws of nature, as we know them, cannot have operated: a Creation in fact.'[6]

Creation here means that event, incomprehensible to science, by which were established the initial conditions of the world. But perhaps, even if science can say nothing of the cause of these conditions, Christian faith might do so? In 1951, Pope Pius XII fell into the trap, saying of Whittaker's ideas that 'science has confirmed the contingency of the Universe and also the well-founded deduction as to the epoch when the cosmos came forth from the hands of the Creator. Therefore, God exists!'[7]

In due time, however, some scientists suggested that the universe is not best thought of as proceeding from some single sharp-edged boundary or point, requiring further explanation. In Hawking's own preferred account, there are 'no singularities at which the laws of science broke down and no edge of space-time at which we would have to appeal to God or some new law to set the boundary conditions of space-time'.[8] God or *some new law*; there could hardly be a clearer illustration of the assumption that the concept of God is supposed to serve as a principle of explanation.

Hawking makes the same mistake as Pius XII but makes it in the opposite direction. The scientist supposes that, in a cosmos without 'edges', the question of God creating would not arise. The pope supposes that, if some set of initial conditions *is* at the 'edge' of scientific understanding, the question of God creating not only arises but receives its answer. But when, in our uses of the Creed, we confess our faith in God, creator of heaven and earth, we are making no claims about, offering no explanations for, the initial conditions of the universe. What *are* we doing? It is time to go back to the beginning!

'The earth was without form and void, and darkness was upon the face of the deep.' The story moves from confusion into clarity, from shapelessness to form and order. The new feature of the Jewish story, later inherited by Christianity as well, was the rejection of the dualisms which see the world as warfare of good and evil forces struggling for supremacy. The God who speaks in Genesis is responsible for everything: for sun and moon, for earth and plants, winged birds and great sea monsters, men and women. All are his creatures and everything, he sees, is work well done. The point I want to emphasize, at present, is that God makes everything, and makes it without effort; not by conquest, but by speech.

Christianity, in due course, added a precision. God makes everything, not only effortlessly, but *ex nihilo*, out of nothing.[9] The effect of this quite crucial clarification is to rule out the possibility that the concept of God may properly serve as a principle of explanation. Explanations are stories of causes and effects. There is no causal story which could start with 'Nothing'. From 'nothing', there is no move the mind could make (what would the next sentence be?). To confess that God creates the world *ex nihilo* is thereby to acknowledge that there is an end to explanation, that it makes no more sense to seek for 'ultimate' explanations of the world that it would to ask what the 'solution' was to the 'plot' of the world's history. (God is, admittedly, still spoken of as cause in the tradition but, here as elsewhere in theology, those who used this language well knew that they were bending familiar notions, metaphorically, to strange new uses.)

To confess the world to be created out of nothing is to acknowledge its contingency. But, from contingency, nothing follows. Here we are. This is how things are. That's it. No safety belts, no metacosmic maps or guidebooks, no mental cradles for our 'ultimate' security. The recognition of contingency, what Schleiermacher called the sense of absolute dependence, may (like vertigo) be intermittently exhilarating, but its more lasting moods lie somewhere between sheer mind-stopped awe and starkest terror.

God may not be participant in the struggles of good and evil which the myths describe; he may make what he makes quite effortlessly; but, in itself, this does not necessarily seem good news for us. God is creator of heaven and earth, of (as the Nicene Creed puts it) all things visible and invisible. God therefore makes, not just the furniture of the idyllic landscape which the Genesis accounts describe, but those unyielding laws and forces – of gravity and economics, entropy and institutional inertia, genetic consequence and the destructive turbulence set in motion by seemingly quite trivial distant human acts – which bind the world so tightly into patterns and structures of seemingly inexorable necessity. The sense of 'absolute' dependence may be quite unnerving but even the multiple bleak bonds of *relative* dependence – of need and duty, poverty, ill-health and loneliness – are enough to give to creaturehood the character not of sonship but of slavery.

The world we live in is not only dark, but dangerous. The people who wrote the first chapters of the book of Genesis knew hunger and injustice, the failure of harvests and the disruption warfare brings, incurable diseases and the cruelty of kings. Yet they had slowly learned that this was not the way, in principle, that the world would be. And, in the paradise stories, they expressed their trust in God who, having brought them through the desert out of Egypt, would bring the people in their land from confusion into order, from turbulence to peace. The tales are told of 'the beginning', but, in order to interpret them, we need to have our eyes fixed, as they did, on the end.

Paradise, or utopia, is differently located in its different versions. If Genesis speaks, apparently, of how things were once upon a time, the eleventh chapter of Isaiah tells how the world eventually will be when the little child leads calf and lion, there is no danger on God's holy mountain, and 'the earth shall be full of the knowledge of God as the waters cover the sea'.[10] The subject-matter of protologies, or tales of the beginning, and eschatologies, or stories of the end, is usually the same. (This raises the question, which I shall consider in the third section of this chapter, as to whether we ought not say that it is in the *end* that God creates the world.) Against the pain and terror of the times they live in, people give narrative form to their conviction that we need not simply settle – whether in Stoic resignation or despair – for such bleak circumstance; that violence, un-meaning and disorder do no have the last word – or the first.

Paradise tales, like other stories, are often badly told. Undisciplined and self-indulgent, they may be little more than fantasies of escapist egotism, speculations born of unacknowledged terror. In modern Western culture, which usually locates its paradise at the end, rather than the beginning, many such stories are classified as science fiction. And the most dangerous form of science fiction is that found in supposedly serious scientific works, especially in the last chapter. Much of this material, apparently motivated by quite old-fashioned dread of death, of life, of flesh, spins pathological fantasies of mankind escaping from all earthly problems, mastering the world, and all this being done – without a thought for moral transformation – either through convenient mathematical necessity or as the outcome of technical dexterity. Thus, according to the physicist Paul Davies, 'with the superforce unleashed, we could change the structures of space and time, tie our own knots in nothingness, and build matter to order . . . truly, we should be lords of the universe'.[11]

'In the beginning God created the heavens and the earth.'[12] In order for stories of creation, tales of world-making or cosmogony, to be realistic, it is of first importance that there is not, either in their telling or their interpretation, any evasion of the darkness of the world or of the desperate nature of the planet's plight; of the conjunction of sheer contingency and seemingly inexorable fate, chance and necessity; of the pervasiveness of structured greed and pain and impotence and terror. I have suggested, in this section, that the doctrine of creation *ex nihilo* points us precisely in the direction of such realism. It follows, of course, that the announcement that it is out of nothing that heaven and earth are made is not, in itself, good news. But it is not necessarily bad news either. It is ambivalent, indecipherable. We do not know quite what to make of it.

Which brings us back to the beginning. This chapter is about 'The Father almighty, creator of heaven and earth'. So far, I have said little of 'almightiness' and nothing about 'Father'. Nor have we reflected yet on quite what 'heaven' and 'earth' might mean. We have not yet, in other words, considered either the manner of God's making or (in any detail) what it is he makes. We have so far concentrated simply on createdness, and on the fact that God makes everything.

But 'creator', we remember, like 'almighty', is a word we use of *God* and not immediately, or primarily, of any one of the three 'persons' that God is. In contrast, the questions to be considered in the next two sections – namely: *how* does God create? and, *what* is the work he does? – are questions which call for more explicitly and directly trinitarian treatment, for the short answers to them would be, first, through his Word or Son and, secondly, ordered harmony in Love. In other words, creatorship considered in abstraction from the sending of the Son and breathing of the Spirit is systematically ambivalent. And the more general lesson to be learned from this would be that what were known, technically, as 'essential' (as distinct from 'personal' – proper to one of the three persons) properties or attributes of God only find their *Christian* sense when considered in relational or 'personal' terms.

It is, accordingly, too early in our reflections on the Creed to know quite what to make of all the darkness of the world. One thing is certain: night is not unreal, nor will we later have occasion to pretend that terror is unwarranted. The still point and centre of the world's creation is what went on one Friday afternoon when, from the sixth hour to the ninth, 'there was darkness over all the land'.[13]

2. Sonship

'"Lord, teach us to pray, as John taught his disciples." And he said to them, "When you pray, say: Father, hallowed be thy name. Thy kingdom come."'[14] It is, then, possible to speak to God, to make requests of God, to give praise to God as one who does things well. The idea is so familiar that it is difficult to appreciate quite what an extraordinary idea it is.

Anthropomorphism, depicting God as rather like a human being, may seem fine for children, or people we consider less sophisticated than ourselves, but for adults? Consider a little of the work we do in our diverse and fragmentary attempts to work the world and find our way around: as economists and engineers, as particle physicists

and planning officers, as novelists and neurosurgeons, ornitho-
logists and obstetricians, molecular biologists and management
consultants. Gather these fragments, in imagination, into some
kind of whole, and then address the mystery of which all this is but
the effortless effect as 'Father'. There is no better corrective to the
flippancy of so much easy speech concerning God than to remember
that the doctrine of the world's createdness is the primary context in
which we call God 'Father', and do so with heads bowed in prayer.

God is not 'a person', for a person would be an individual with a
nature, a thing of some particular kind – which is what creatures are.
Nor, as we have seen, is God three persons – if that description
carries connotations of God being something like three people. Yet
Christians, like Jews and Muslims, speak of God, in personal terms,
knowing and loving what he freely makes. Perhaps especially here,
however, we need to keep in mind how little we understand the
sense of what we say when stretching our language across the chasm
between God's being and ours.

That heaven and earth are made from nothing is not, in itself, as
we have seen, good news. What makes the doctrine of createdness
good news is the discovery that God makes the world 'parentally'.
'Father of things tangible and things unseen.'[15] In the Jewish and
Christian tradition we first learned to call God 'Father' by coming to
understand his ordering of the world he makes after the manner of
beneficent and effective kingship. 'Father . . . thy kingdom come' is
thus a prayer for the completion of God's creative work.

If all creation is God's 'child', the sense of this found focus in a
people's recognition of election sustained in spite of waywardness:
'When Israel was a child, I loved him, and out of Egypt I called my
son . . . The more I called them, the more they went from me . . . Yet
it was I who taught Ephraim to walk, I took them up in my arms . . .
and I bent down to them and fed them.' Eventually, in Christianity,
the final intensification of this imagery finds creation finished in a
human being (an '*adam*'), no longer wayward, the history of whose
production transcribes in space and time the act of 'generation' that
is God's own self. If Jesus of Nazareth may properly be called 'the
first-born among many brethren',[16] then human being and, perhaps,
all of creaturely existence, is brought within the very life of God.

It is often said, these days, that it is not the obsolete character of the imagery of kingly rule which makes the language of God's 'fatherhood' difficult to use so much as, on the one hand, the fact that what many people know of fatherhood is so little, or so unbearable, as to make talk of *God's* fatherhood at best questionable and, at worst, obscene and, on the other hand, the reinforcement of 'patriarchal' prejudice which is more or less inevitable if the theme of God's parenthood is never, or hardly ever, worked out in the language of maternity.

Concerning these not unrelated issues, there are at least the following four points to be made. In the first place, while the experience on which we draw in our attempts to speak of God may be familiar to us, God is not. What we say of God is only appropriately said if said with care, and delicacy, and a sense of the vast silence that surrounds our speech. There is nothing whatsoever that God is 'obviously' like, and certainly not us!

Moreover, in the second place, using familiar categories to speak of God is not a matter of saying: You know, of course, what kingship and shepherding, landowning and loving, fatherhood and judgeship are? Well, that is how God is and acts. On the contrary, throughout the Scriptures, and by no means only in the prophetic writings, a deeper current flows, according to which God is declared to be precisely *not* a king or shepherd, landowner or lover, judge or father, as the others are. The things we say of God are said in criticism of our inhuman, and hence ungodly, practices. Unlike other judges, God judges justly; unlike other shepherds, God brings back the strayed, binds up the crippled, and strengthens the weak; unlike other fathers, God acts like the father in the misnamed parable of the prodigal son (to which we shall return).[17] It is, therefore, only through the redemptive transformation of our human practices that we discover what these images might mean when used as metaphors for our relation to the unknown God.

What the Scriptures say at length, the Creed says briefly. To confess our faith in God as 'Father' is therefore to be committed to the reform of all those practices and institutions – economic, political and ecclesial – which prevent us not only from experiencing the manner of God's 'parenting' in our relationships with each other, but also from exhibiting, as creatures made to 'image' God, something of God's style of parenting in turn.

In the third place, neither in Scripture nor in classical trinitarian theology is emphasis laid on God as Father and *not*, or as distinct from, Mother. An illustration of how difficult it is to dislodge assumptions to the contrary is provided by our failure to notice passages in which God is depicted in maternal terms; an example would be the passage from Hosea which I quoted earlier. This seems, evidently, to be an image of a mother and her child. In most of the commentaries, this is not denied – it is just that the possibility seems never to have crossed the commentator's mind!

Fourth and finally, encroaching a little on the subject-matter of the second article of the Creed in order to illuminate the sense of 'Father' in the first, let me briefly indicate some implications of the doctrine of Jesus' divine sonship. Jesus was, as we all are, a product of nature and of history. As such a product, he was destructible and was, indeed, destroyed. We are none of us, however, *merely* products. We are not only produced; we are also, in different ways, and with most varied efficacy, cherished. There are few human beings of whom someone has not, at some time, even fleetingly, been fond. But, quite apart from the fact that many people are little loved, and loved with little selflessness and effective care, even the purest and most effective human loving cannot prevent the destruction, cannot transcend the mortality, of the products that we are.

To declare Jesus to be Son of *God* is to declare that he was not only produced, but unswerving, indestructibly, 'absolutely' cherished. If we take 'loving production' to be part of what we mean by 'parenthood' and if, in declaring Jesus to be Son of *God*, we declare parenthood to be an attribute of God, we are thereby declaring our conviction, derived from reflection on his fate, that being lovingly produced, being effectively cherished with a love which transcends destruction in mortality, is part of what it means and will be to be human (for he is the 'first-born of many brethren'). It follows that to confess Jesus to be Son of God declares our confidence in his resurrection and our hope for the resurrection of all humankind. If 'parenthood' is an attribute of God, then the destruction of the product is not the last word concerning the condition of the world.

I earlier suggested, as an implication of God's 'almightiness', his sole sovereignty of the world he makes *ex nihilo*, that, in contrast to those divinities enmeshed in energetic metacosmic struggle, of uncertain outcome, between the forces of good and evil, God makes the world quite effortlessly: all he does is *speak*. When, however, we consider (as I am doing in this section) the first article of the Creed from the standpoint of the subject matter of the second, it soon becomes apparent that this way of putting it will not quite do. God creates in freedom, for there is nothing 'outside' God that could constrain his act: *ex nihilo* God makes the world. But, making it, announcing it, giving finite, particular expression to the eternal Word, is not uncostly. That is the side of things I now want briefly to consider.

Perhaps the place to start is with Paul's image of the entire history of the world as an act of painful birth: 'the whole creation has been groaning in travail together until now; and not only the creation but we ourselves, who have the first fruits of the Spirit, groan inwardly as we wait for adoption as sons, the redemption of our bodies'. Yet this adoption is not simply future, for 'When we cry, "Abba! Father!" it is the Spirit himself bearing witness within our spirit that we are children of God and, if children, then ... fellow heirs with Christ, provided we suffer with him.' It is true that the motif of birth is intertwined with that of punishment, echoing Genesis 3, but the emphasis is on the labour rather than the occasion of its cause. Most remarkably, that same breath of God that hovered over primal chaos now breathes in us the possibility of prayer 'with sighs too deep for words'.[18]

There is another line running from Genesis 3 which points in the same direction. A late Isaian psalm tells us that one consequence of the people's lethargy and lack of zeal is that God's work in them, safeguarding their city and expanding its frontiers, is experienced by them 'as a woman with child, who writhes and cries out in her pangs, when she is near her time'. This passage is picked up in the Fourth Gospel: 'When a woman is in travail she has sorrow, because her hour has come; but when she is delivered of the child, she no longer remembers the anguish, for joy that a child [better: "a human being"; the Greek has *anthropos*] is born into the world. So you have sorrow now, but I will see you again and your hearts will rejoice.'[19] Many commentators, ancient, and modern, have detected Adamic overtones in that '*anthropos*': the outcome of present suffering (Jesus' passion and the disciples' 'sorrow') will be the achievement of the birth of humankind, the finishing of God's creative work.

Finally, it is worth mentioning that when, in his study of the Trinity, Augustine introduces the theme (so central to his story) of the Fall, the figure in which he does so is not protological but existential, in a series of allusions to the parable of the prodigal son. The human mind, which 'turns away from [God] and slithers and slides down into less and less which is imagined to be more and more', may still retain a trace in memory 'which has not deserted it on its travels to far countries' of the vision of 'some excellent end, that is its own security and happiness', and therewith be turned back towards self-knowledge and the knowledge of God. The whole drama of humankind is thus presented as a homecoming into the waiting arms of God.[20] (I said earlier that the parable is misnamed: the central figure, as the commentators all agree, is the father's unconditioned and unswerving love.)

In the first section of this chapter, I concluded that the doctrine of God's creatorship, considered in abstraction from the Word through whose utterance and the Spirit whose outbreathing the work is done, was systematically ambivalent. In this second section, therefore, we have concentrated on the *manner* of God's creation which – according to the Scriptures as focussed in the Creed – is 'parental'. If, in order to take things one step further, we set together the biblical themes and images that I have included, then I am inclined to say that the strong and central Jewish doctrine of the endlessly generous fidelity of God (one form of which is the Jewish, and then the Christian, doctrine of God's fatherhood) is, in the trinitarian development of Christianity, radicalized in the direction of a maternal understanding of how the Creator in due time brings the world to birth through the laborious bearing of her Son in love.

'... what he sees the Father doing'

I earlier endorsed the classic rule of speech, in trinitarian theology, according to which the three there are in God are only to be distinguished from each other in terms of the 'relationships of origin' which they are said to be. Thus, for example, we distinguish 'uttering' from 'being word', 'fathering' from 'being son', but this does not entitle us to speak (for instance) as if the Father and the Son were two different people with two minds or hearts or wills.

At once, however, a difficulty looms, a problem which has caused endless expenditure of ink and energy. I include what some may find too technical a note about this problem because, although not bearing directly on the topic of creation, it does have implications for the restraint, or lack of it, with which we handle the anthropomorphisms that are inevitable in our attempts to speak of God and, in particular, of God as 'Father' and as 'Son'.

The difficulty I have in mind arises from the fact that Jesus Christ, the Word incarnate, the one 'sent' by God, *is* a 'person' in the quite straightforward sense of being a human being with a mind, and heart, and will. And so we may entertain an image, of Jesus on his knees in prayer (in Gethsemane, perhaps) addressing God as 'Father'. The Son gazes upwards, in the dark, towards the Father, who gazes down, in silence that is hard to bear, upon the Son. What, in evoking such an image, we are liable to overlook is that in constructing it we have blended or confused the straightforward fact of Jesus' human personhood with the *metaphor* of 'Son' and 'Father' which we use to indicate a distinction within the mystery of God. Jesus has eyes. How does the Father 'gaze'?

The effect of this confusion soon becomes apparent when theologians turn their attention to the procession of the Spirit. In the West, it was insisted *both* that the Father and the Son are one source or 'principle' of the Spirit – that the Spirit is a single 'gift' or movement within God, *and* that the Spirit is the mutual love 'between' the Father and the Son. It is the imagining of that 'between' which then gets us into difficulties.

The trouble is, to put it very simply, that, if two people love each other, their mutual love – however strong, or deep, or fruitful – has *two* sources or 'principles', not one: the love the first has for the second, and the love the second bears, reciprocally, for the first. Augustine weaves endless and ingenious variations on the theme that love 'couples' or 'unites' or 'binds together' utterance and uttered word, memory and understanding, the Father and the Son. And yet the logic of such images ineluctably requires that there be two from whom love springs; two to be coupled, or bound together, or united. In other words, images of two things mutually attracted or of two people in love make it impossible for coherent expression to be given to the idea that the first and second 'persons' in the Trinity are one single source or principle of the procession of the third.

In Augustine's writings on the Trinity, the image of the Spirit as the love 'between' the Father and the Son exists alongside, and in tension with, the far more fruitful metaphor of the Spirit as the love consequent upon self-knowledge, the 'delight' which utterance of a good word brings. But this family of metaphors, which has no need of any talk of love 'between' or 'joining' that from which it springs, influential as it was on later theology, may seem at first sight to leave our initial difficulty untouched. It is, perhaps ironically, Augustine himself who supplies the elements for its solution.

'The Son can do nothing of his own accord, but only what he see the Father doing.' But what does it mean to say that the Son 'sees' the Father's work? Sight is, of course (and especially in the Fourth Gospel) a metaphor for understanding, for 'seeing the point'. And it is this which gives Augustine just the clue he needs. Jesus is the incarnation of that pure 'from-the-fatherness' which is God's Word or Son: 'The work of Father and Son is indivisible, and yet the Son's working is from the Father just as he himself is from the Father; and *the way in which the Son sees the Father is simply by being the Son*. For him, being from the Father, that is being born of the Father, is not something different from seeing the Father.' Or, as he put it in his commentary on the Fourth Gospel: '*Videndo enim natus est, et nascendo videt*'; 'In seeing he is born, and in being born he sees'.[21] In Gethsemane, Jesus still sees the Father, knows himself even into this world's darkness being born.

3. Harmony

It is out of nothing that all things are made by one who has no rival in their making. To these bare bones of the doctrine of divine creation I added, in the second section of this chapter, some remarks from the standpoint of the second article of the Creed; from the standpoint, that is to say, of one in whose light we learn that God creates parentally, brings all things to birth in patient and forgiving love. I have, in other words, said something of the world's createdness and of the manner in which God's work is done. But I have so far said almost nothing of what it is God makes. The focus in this final section, therefore, is on 'heaven and earth'.

The section might have been entitled 'order', for God's creating is, undoubtedly, an 'ordering'. It is an ordering both in the sense in which order is contrasted with *dis*order, and in the more metaphorical but no less important sense in which what happens occurs because God orders it: says 'Let it be so'. Nevertheless, it seemed to me that 'order' is too neutral a term, too formal, sufficiently to help us keep in mind that it is parentally, in kindness and unswerving care, that God's work is done. Moreover, to speak of 'order' does not make it clear enough that, in this section, we are considering the doctrine of creation from the standpoint of the third article of the Creed. 'Harmony' indicates more directly than does 'order' that it is God's work as *outcome* which is our immediate concern: the inhabitation or indwelling of God's own self or Spirit in what God does. 'Order' might be mistaken for mere tidiness, whereas 'harmony' speaks more immediately not only of the beauty of God's work but also of its character as reconciliation.

To confess belief in God is to pledge our lives, our minds, our hearts, in God's direction. We could not do this without at least some preliminary idea of what our place is in God's work and of what it is we have to do. We are a part of 'heaven and earth', perhaps the only part to bear a measure of responsibility for what happens. In other words, although the topics to be treated in this section will be considered in more detail later on (and especially in Chapter VI), without some mention of them here I would not sufficiently have indicated what is entailed in confessing our faith in the creation of the world by God.

What does God make? God makes all things, in heaven and on earth. God makes the world. But what do we take the constituents of the world to be? What kinds of thing does God create when he creates the world? The standard answers, these days, to such questions, tend mostly to make mention of inorganic matter: whirling gases, deep seas and rock formations, galaxies and stars. 'Life' may be mentioned, but probably in some rather vague and general way, and, if human being finds any place upon the list at all, it is only as the outcome of one small strand in the processes of evolution.

Most people, in other words, think of creation as the making of the world which the natural sciences describe.

The most amazing omission from such accounts is the world of human culture: of rituals and relationships, of languages and symbol systems, trade and agriculture. On all such matters, most modern treatments of the doctrine of creation are strangely silent. Does not God make cities as well as stars? Is God's self-gift, the Spirit's presence, less intimately and immediately constitutive of promises and symphonies than of plutonium and silt? These are not trick questions, but some of our assumptions may make them seem so, assumptions which have to do, first, with the distinctions that we draw between human beings and other creatures and, secondly, with our understanding of the relationship between God's agency and ours.

Notice, in the first place, then, how easily we draw distinctions between the 'human' and the 'natural' worlds, as if we (or, at least, some bit of us) formed no part of nature. Helped by theories of the human self or 'soul' which owe little or nothing to the Scriptures or to Aristotle (whom I mention as a reminder that we may not blame, for our bad habits, people vaguely referred to as 'the Greeks'), we speak and act as if 'we' were, not part of creation, but creation's lords, 'godlets' entitled to manipulate and use the world as private property.

Against all such dissociations of the human from the natural, of mind from body, of culture from creation, I only wish (at this point) to insist that the warrants for them may not be found in Scripture. What does God make? The short answer, according to the Scriptures, is that God makes an ordered world, an harmonious place, in which his people dwell in peace. Thus, for example, Psalm 104 begins with the stretching of the heavens like a tent and the making of the clouds to be God's chariot, moves through the provision of springs in the valleys, grass for the cattle, and bread and wine to strengthen and gladden human hearts, and ends with the wicked getting their come-uppance – observed by the rest of us with a certain satisfaction from a safe distance!

Nowhere in the Old Testament is God's creation, his ordering of things, presented as an instantaneous achievement. In Isaiah, for example, cosmogony or world-making and exodus-conquest form a single theme. It is through the redemptive labour of pacifying chaos, overthrowing enemies, and rescuing from threats of every kind, that God creates the world in which his people safely dwell. The same pattern is at work in the best known of all Old Testament creation material, the early chapters of the Book of Genesis. The entire section which runs from 2.4 to 11.26 has been so edited as to constitute a single tale of world-making. The unifying thread is the repeated phrase 'These are the generations' – the makings-to-be – of 'the heavens and the earth', of the human being ('Adam'), of Noah, of his sons, and of Abram's father. Thus, the sweep of God's one generative, world-making work reaches from the cosmic context to the nations and, at last, to Israel. That is what God makes.[22]

Nor is this pattern, of one work achieved in the harmonious existence of God's people, abandoned when we come to the New Testament. From Colossians to Hebrews and the Fourth Gospel, God's one work of creation is seen as founded, and focussed, and finished, in him through whom all things are made (what an extraordinary claim this is) and in the peace eventually achieved 'by the blood of his cross'.[23]

There are two lessons that I would draw from this. The first is that, although we need (for reasons that will become a little clearer when we consider the mystery of sin) conceptually to distinguish the making from the healing of the world, 'creation' from 'redemption' and 'sanctification', these are best thought of as three aspects of a single process, of one work done in the Spirit through the Word, and not as three different processes, three different acts that God does in succession. (I would, at this point, refer the reader back to my outline, at the end of Chapter III, of trinitarian rules for reading the Apostles' Creed.) The second lesson would be that, in a culture such as ours which finds eschatology easier to handle than protology and which, moreover, tends to confuse the doctrine of the world's createdness with enquiries concerning the initial conditions of the universe, we may quite seriously mislead ourselves and other people if we continue simply to reiterate that it is 'in the beginning' that God creates the heavens and the earth. At the very least, we need to keep in mind that, as confession of faith in the Creator, as acknowledgment of our and all things' absolute and immediate dependence on the mystery in which we live and move and have our being, and at the service of whose ordering of all things in harmony we pledge ourselves wholeheartedly to work, this is the *same* answer as that also given, in the New Testament as in the Old, when it is said that God comes to dwell with us, makes us at home with him, inhabits us, in the *end*. Paradise is God's finished work.

Does not God make cities as well as stars, symphonies as well as silt? The second set of assumptions which lead us to suspect some sleight-of-hand in questions such as these concerns the relationship between God's agency and ours. How is the recognition of our absolute and immediate dependence upon God compatible with our sense of human dignity and freedom, responsibility and guilt? If God creates this text that I write now, shapes the thoughts and sets the words in order, then how is this text *mine*? Such questions matter, for behind them lies an even more disturbing one: if God does all the things I do, then what is left of me? And yet, if these things are not done by God, then God does not make all the things there are; is not, after all, 'creator of heaven and earth'.

If God were an object in the world, a force or thing whose agency or power could, at least in principle, thwart our ambitions, threaten our freedom, obliterate our identity, then all our fears would be well-warranted. We are finite things, products of place and time and circumstance, ephemeral and minute specks in networks of cause and consequence beyond imagining. We are not very large, or very powerful, or even (save to ourselves) very interesting. Our dreams are limited, our deeds hemmed in, by natural and social forces far stronger and more ingenious than ourselves. We are, moreover, not only small and weak, but unreliable. And so are all the others, growth in dependence upon whom is, therefore, always dangerous: they dominate or let you down, they disappear or die.

Finitude, then, is frightening enough but, at first sight, at least, createdness seems worse. Finite things are products, dependent on the causes that produce them and the circumstances in which they find themselves. Createdness, however, is a matter of *absolute* dependence, for it is from *nothing* that each and every breath and movement, muscle and heartbeat, prayer and cry of pain or longing, is, at every moment, made. We are, accordingly, either quite unreal, figments of some dark god's sadism, or ... what?

As we saw in the first section of this chapter, the doctrine of creation out of nothing is not, in itself, good news. We do not know quite what to make of it. We are, however, provided, in the Creed, with a pattern or framework for its interpretation; a pattern according to which we learn not only that God creates parentally but also that to be a creature is to be indwelt, inhabited, by the gift of God's own self. It follows, according to the Christian construal of createdness, that it is in an absolute dependence upon the unknown mystery of God that we find not only our existence and identity, but our cherishing and forgiveness, our flourishing and peace.

How on earth might we discover this improbable suggestion to be not only plausible but true? Clearly not by logical dexterity or imaginative ingenuity alone, for the best efforts of poets and philosophers would leave untouched the dark and actual witness of experience, in which 'dependence' is not a noble term, evoking (as it does) the squalor and banality of our inhumanness; the carelessness of slavery and degradation; the pervasiveness of domination, and disease, and death.

What we call Christianity is supposed to be a kind of school the purpose of whose pedagogy is to foster the conditions in which dependence might be relearned as friendship; conditions in which the comprehensive taming of chaos by loving order, of conflict by tranquillity, of discord by harmony, might be instantiated and proclaimed. To use the Creed, to make its articles one's own, is, therefore, to be pledged in labour towards the kind of 'heaven and earth' in which our human work might be the finite form of God's.

V

Appearing

'I believe in Jesus Christ, his only Son, our Lord.
He was conceived by the power of the Holy Spirit
  and born of the Virgin Mary.
He suffered under Pontius Pilate,
  was crucified, died, and was buried.
He descended to the dead.
On the third day he rose again.
He ascended into heaven,
  and is seated at the right hand of the Father.
He will come again to judge the living and the dead.'

In an earlier chapter, making somewhat guarded reference to 'the
narrative character of the Creed', I said that the way things hang
together, in the Christian scheme of things, has more in common
with the oneness of a story with a single plot than with the oneness of
a list of objects of belief.[1] Nevertheless, it must be admitted that the
Apostles' Creed is not, at least on the surface of its text, straight-
forwardly narrative in form. Although the order of the articles
reflects the story that we tell of God, and of what God does that is
not God – a tale of a world made through uttered Word and
outbreathed Spirit – this narrative remains implicit. The articles, in
fact, are simply set in sequence, echoing the threefold questioning
of the baptismal liturgies (an effect now heightened, in the ICET
translation, by the repetition of 'I believe' in the second article as
well as in the third). Moreover, of the three articles, only the second
(to which we now turn) is set out in narrative form. Confessing our
faith in Jesus Christ, we first say who he is and then, in six brief
steps, we summarize his story, say how it went with him.

What seems to have happened is that, perhaps as early as the end of the second century AD, two originally independent types of credal summary were joined together: the threefold baptismal confession and the kind of 'short story' declaration of good news informal versions of which abound in the New Testament.[2] If, then, we take the second part of the article, from 'He was conceived' to 'judge the living and the dead', as sketching such a story, we need to ask: *what* story or stories does it summarize? What is the plot? Where does it begin and end? What the Scriptures say at length, the Creed says briefly. But the New Testament interprets Jesus' identity and role, tells the story of him whom we confess as Christ, in a number of different ways. If we overlook these differences, or try to blend them all together into some single tale, the effect is simply to obscure from view the *actual* message proclaimed by each of them in its own way, and by all of them together. In establishing its rule of faith, or 'canon', the church took *four* Gospels, not any one of them alone. Thus, even overlooking (simply for the sake of illustration) the important differences within the Synoptic tradition, the contrast is striking between those strands in that tradition which portray Jesus as 'a man whose death was followed by resurrection and exaltation at God's right hand, where he would appear on the clouds at the end of time as the divinely appointed judge', and the picture which emerges in the Fourth Gospel of 'one who had come down to earth from heaven; he would carry out his role as judge while on earth and return to heaven'.[3]

Against this background, it is clear that the story summarized in the second article of the Apostles' Creed is closer to the Synoptics than to John (whereas the Nicene draws more or less equally on both traditions). However, any suggestion that, therefore, the Fourth Gospel is a less authoritative guide than the Synoptics in our attempts to understand the Creed would be contradicted by two thousand years of Christian practice. In this chapter I shall, for reasons to be indicated in due course, stay closer to the Fourth Gospel than to the Synoptics. But, first, some brief comments on the individual clauses which make up this second article of the Creed.

'... *Jesus Christ*'. It is, by now, quite difficult for us to keep in mind that 'Christ' is a title and not a proper name. To speak of Jesus as Messiah, or Christ, as God's anointed, is to locate him in a history of Jewish expectation. Therefore, even though being a Christian does not entail being a Jew, to appropriate this title in a Christian creed is to locate *ourselves*, as well, within the perspectives of that same history; is to make Israel's memories our own and to shape our hope for humankind to contours which Israel first formed. Thus, for example, it simple makes no sense to confess Jesus to be Christ while seldom if ever taking the psalms and the prophetic writings as substance of one's prayer.

'*his only Son, our Lord*'. As in the Fourth Gospel, that 'only' reflects the process whereby the sense of 'Son of God', once a messianic title without connotations of divinity, was gradually focussed to bear the weight of the conviction that, in this one human being, God's own self finds full expression in our world. It would not do to say that, unlike the rest of us, Jesus is 'literally' God's Son, for this might lead us to forget that *all* our talk of 'parenting' in God is, unavoidably and evidently, metaphorical. We are here, of course, at the heart of issues which racked the church in controversy during the period of the creeds' formation. Then, it was said that, whereas the rest of us are 'made', 'adopted', even, in his Spirit, 'born', he alone is, from the beginning, *simply* 'born': '*genitum, non factum*'; 'begotten, not made', as the Nicene Creed has it.

'*He was conceived by the power of the Holy Spirit and born of the Virgin Mary*'. Until around the middle of the fourth century, this clause usually read: 'born by [*de*] the Holy Spirit from [*ex*] the Virgin Mary'. Whatever the exact motives which led to the elaboration 'conceived by the Holy Spirit, born of the Virgin Mary', it has the effect of drawing more firmly the distinction between God's act and Mary's motherhood.[4] I do not know why, or on what authority, ICET decided to insert 'the power of'. Perhaps they wished to ward off the kind of crude misunderstanding which would make of Christ a mythological superman: half human, half divine.

This was no ordinary birth. God's full enfleshment, definitive appearance, in our world, is not an act or happening like any other. It is, entirely, God's act, God's fulfilment of the promise, God's 'templing' presence in his people, performed through Israel's faith. This, in one version or another, is the story told in Matthew and in Luke, in Paul's letter to the Galatians and in the Prologue to the

Fourth Gospel. For Luke and Matthew, the story finds focus in the image of the fruitful virgin, which does not figure in Mark's version or in John's.

The primary task of understanding what we are called on to confess in this article of the Creed is made more difficult by preoccupation with the secondary question of whether or not Jesus had a human father. In calling this question secondary, I do not mean that it is unimportant. I only mean, as Cardinal Ratzinger once put it, that 'the doctrine of Jesus' divinity would not be affected if Jesus had been the product of a normal human marriage'.[5] In other words: confessing Jesus to be Son of *God* most certainly does not entail denying that he was any other father's son.

The infancy narratives are richly woven tapestries of Old Testament allusion.[6] They have little direct value as evidence of what went on before and after Jesus' birth, and such historical evidence as they *do* afford bears primarily on Mary's faith and Jesus' humanness. The fourth eucharistic prayer in the present Roman liturgy contains the sentence: 'He was conceived through the power of the Holy Spirit and born of the Virgin Mary; a man like us in all things but sin.' This, says Raymond Brown, catches 'the precise thrust of the credal confession'.[7]

The nerve-centre of some people's fears in this matter concerns the reliability of Christian tradition. That Jesus had no human father has been believed so widely, so consistently, so confidently, and for so long, that calling it in question appears to threaten the foundation of our confidence in the message we receive and are invited to proclaim.

Although such nervousness is entirely understandable, it moves too fast. To repeat the point I made about the primary and secondary issues: if the question of Mary's biological virginity becomes more important, in piety or preaching, than the question of her faith, her dispossession, the single-mindedness of her obedience to God, and than the full-fleshed presence in our world of God which this faith brings to birth, then something has gone badly wrong. The consistent heart and centre of the doctrine of what is usually called 'the virgin birth', as expounded by Augustine and Aquinas, by Luther and by Calvin – and by countless others who believed, as these four did, that Jesus had no human father –

has been the conviction that the birth of the Messiah is due wholly to God's agency, to God's deed done through the instrumental agency of Mary's faith.

Thus, for example, in a sermon on the Apostles' Creed, preached to catechumens, Augustine said of Mary: 'By believing, she conceived him whom she bore for our belief'; and, in the same sermon: 'Filled with faith, conceiving Christ in her mind before doing so in her womb, she said: "Behold, I am the handmaid of the Lord; let it be to me according to your word".'[8] God's Word fleshed in faith that welcomes it: *that* is the message of this clause in the Creed.

In distinguishing, as I have done, between the image bearing the belief and the interpretation of that image as literal description of the manner of Mary's motherhood, I am not suggesting that what happened in the past forms no part of Christian confession. If the first article of the Creed sweeps heaven and earth, confessing the createdness of all things that are and have been and will ever be, this second article is focussed on one small point in space and time; on one individual human being and how it went with him. The clause which bears this burden is not, however, the one that we have been considering, but the one that follows it.

'*He suffered under Pontius Pilate, was crucified, died, and was buried.*' 'Suffered' and 'died' are relatively late additions to the Creed, appearing, as they do, in the fifth and sixth centuries respectively. Both terms were, of course, part of every Christian teacher's stock-in-trade from the beginning, and their inclusion (which may have been motivated, at least in part, by the need continually to insist that Jesus was a human being, 'like us in all things' except resistance to the Father's will) hardly calls for comment.

On the other hand, it is worth remarking how laconic this clause is. We go straight from birth to death. There is no mention made of any teaching, as if it were elsewhere than in words that the weight of God's Word's utterance lies (we shall return to this). And, in our use of the Apostles' Creed, we do not even proclaim *why* Jesus died (in contrast to the Nicene Creed, which says that these things were done 'for us', '*pro nobis*'). No doctrine here, no ethics, no uplifting thoughts; merely the mention of one man's suffering and death, 'under Pontius Pilate'.

With the inclusion of these three words, 'arguably the only genuinely historical element in the Christian creed', the character of our confession is marked out as quite different from the endorsement of an ideology or system of ideas.[9] Christianity is not a 'worldview', or system of beliefs. It is a people with a memory and, for all the world, a hope.

'*He descended to the dead.*' Although this clause has no equivalent in the Nicene Creed, it probably found its way into Western creeds from the East. Originally simply a corollary of Jesus' death – for was not the grave or pit of Sheol the place to which the dead departed? – it eventually came to serve two rather different purposes. Read as the aftermath of Calvary, it affirms the reality of Jesus' death, indicating that there is no depth, no darkness, no unravelling of reality, which God's Son has not shared – allowing Nicholas of Cusa to speak of 'God's no longer articulable Word'.[10] Read, on the other hand, with hindsight, from the standpoint of Easter, it was interpreted as the beginning of Christ's triumph; his proclamation, to the dead, of life; his 'harrowing of hell', rescuing those stuck in Satan's jaw.

'Descended to the dead' is, arguably, less misleading than 'descended into hell', but ICET's attempt to justify this mistranslation of a word which does, undoubtedly, refer to a place (*inferna*; 'the lower world') on the grounds that 'place of the dead' would have pressed too far the metaphor of descent, is not convincing.[11] If such coyness is necessary in speaking of 'descent', would not the same fastidiousness require that 'rose again' and 'ascended' be similarly watered down?

'*On the third day he rose again. He ascended into heaven, and is seated at the right hand of the Father.*' ICET defends its addition of 'again' (the Latin has simply 'rose' or 'resurrected': '*resurrexit*') on the grounds that it is 'an English colloquialism which is appropriate to the spatial metaphor'.[12] I disagree, for reasons which will indicate why I take this clause together with that on the ascension.

The proclamation of Christ's resurrection is the wellspring, heart and centre of the Christian message. From it, all else radiates; to it, all else points. In its announcement, something new is done, and said, and seen – concerning God, and us, and all the world. It is not therefore surprising that it should find expression, in the New

Testament, in many different images and stories. There are stories which require the absence of Jesus from the scene (stories of the empty tomb, and messages from angels) and others which require his presence (either to send the church out on its way, to proclaim that Jesus is the Christ, or so that the Christ be recognized, with a little difficulty, as Jesus). And, of course, the way in which the light of Easter plays back upon the narratives that went before – of death and teaching, baptism and birth – differs considerably in the different accounts. There simply is no single image into whose contours all this wealth of material can be strait-jacketed in such a way that we could say: and *this* is what is meant by 'resurrection'.

Having issued that warning, it may be safe, though simplifying matters, to suggest that the theme of Christ's glorification is worked out, in the New Testament, through three different kinds of story. There is the Johannine version, according to which the whole story of Christ, from birth to death, is told as the story of the manifestation or appearing of God's glory – culminating on the cross. Secondly, however, the Gospels' contrast between earth and heaven is usually proclaimed, not in such simultaneous but rather in successive terms, as the story of one 'believed on in the world, taken up into glory'. And Paul, like Matthew, tells of the glorified and risen one appearing to those whom he commissions to do God's work.[13] Only in the Lucan narratives do we find that third version of the story which draws a clear distinction between rising from the dead and ascending into heaven.[14] It is not the distinction, in itself, which does the damage, but those versions of it which speak as if Christ first came 'back' to life and then went up to heaven. To my mind, 'rose *again*' risks perpetuating just this kind of misinterpretation.

'Resurrection' and 'ascension' are perhaps best thought of not as two distinct events but rather as two aspects of one message concerning Jesus' destiny and the fate of humankind. In one man's life, and death, and destiny, there is enacted and initiated and displayed the work or deed of God, of whom Hosea said: 'the Lord ... has stricken, and he will bind us up. After two days he will revive us; and on the third day he will raise us up, that we may live before him.'[15] Those laid low by suffering and sin are set back on their feet again before the face of God. (Some languages, such as Danish and

German, have 'upstanding', which holds the metaphor much better than our 'resurrection'.)

There is, of course, a difference between Jesus' destiny and ours. He alone goes up to God as victor and as judge. Thus the first letter of Peter, which says, succinctly, that we are saved 'through the resurrection of Jesus Christ, who has gone into heaven and is at the right hand of God, with angels, authorities, and powers subject to him', picks up a theme first sounded in the Psalms: 'The Lord says to my Lord: "Sit at my right hand, till I make your enemies your footstool." '[16]

One last remark concerning the interpretation of this New Testament material (and, hence, of the clauses in the Creed which say briefly what it says at length). Is the statement 'Jesus is seated at the right hand of the Father' true? Yes. Does the statement express its truth metaphorically? Yes. Few Christians, I think, would be much troubled by this exchange, or by a similar exchange concerning the ascension. Most people know that heaven is not the sky (which is why the icon painters 'painted heaven gold instead of blue').[17] But the theologian who announces that 'he rose again' is also metaphorical is sometimes most unpopular.

'Rose', 'ascended', 'seated'; these are episodes in the story that we tell of Jesus' destiny in God; of how it went with him. But if, as seems reasonable, we limit the scope of our use of the term 'history' to what occurs between the birth and death of human beings and their world and is, at least in principle, subject to our scrutiny, then 'rose', 'ascended', 'seated' are not names for episodes in Jesus' history. What about the empty tomb? If the tomb was empty then, indeed, its emptiness is an historical fact and its emptying an historical event. But that event, even if miraculously wrought, does no more than barely touch the fringe of what 'resurrection' means. To put it in a different figure: if God is invisible, then the invisible is, indeed, of vastly more importance than the visible. The scope of history, however, is limited to things seen. (I have not forgotten, by the way, that the theme of this chapter is our confession of God's *appearing* in the Son or Word. My concern, in these preliminary remarks, is simply to offer a few notes which may help readers take their bearings when interpreting the clauses of this second article of the Creed.)

'*He will come again to judge the living and the dead*.' The Latin says he will come '*inde*', 'thence', come from God's right hand. 'When the Son of man comes in his glory, and all the angels with him, then he will sit on his glorious throne.'[18] This is no messenger or envoy, this human figure on the throne of all creation's king, but the very face of God's almightiness, from whose gaze there is no place to hide. With the exception of the Cross itself, and figures of the the mother with her child, no image has exerted so powerful a hold upon the Christian imagination. By far the best commentaries on this clause of the Creed, to my mind, are the great Romanesque tympana at Conques, and Moissac, and Vézélay. These massive doorways, through which we must pass in order to gain entry to God's house, are considerably more sophisticated, theologically, than Michelangelo's fresco in the Sistine Chapel, where the portrayal of Christ, 'like an antique hero-god', indeed exhibits dominance and power, but quite lacks gentle strength or tranquil majesty.[19]

ICET has added 'again', which is not in the Latin. This is a little unfortunate, because although the emphasis it gives has ample warrant in the Scriptures (and is explicit in the Nicene Creed) it risks slackening that tension between the present and the future without which we lose imaginative purchase on the *singleness* of God's creative and redemptive work. Thus, on the one hand, the sense of futureness, of expectation, heightened by 'again', is quite appropriate because – in a world so bleakly structured in injustice – the Creed proclaims our confidence that justice will one day comprehensively be done: that the last word does not lie with egotism and arbitrary power. On the other hand, the danger with all talk of 'first' and 'second' comings is that, by giving the impression that God, in Christ, is now simply *absent*, it deaden our attentiveness to present signals of God's coming, signs of his presence in the 'times between'.

There is only *one* 'coming forth' from God, the Father, only one procession of God's Word which, in our world, sounds as God's judgment. To be a Christian, or a Jew, is to know that each and every day is that day of which it once was said: 'I set before you this day a blessing and a curse.'[20] Today, and every day, there are choices to be made, choices with incalculable consequence, choices the discernment and execution of which are either forms of the appearance of the justness which is God, or else the darkening form of our refusal. A blessing and a curse: our 'Yes' and 'No' to God. Thus, the first Christians' expectation of an imminent, world-ending, act of God – return 'again' of Christ, modulated not to disappointment but to patient watchfulness. The image on those great French doorways – an image of clear and final resolution – is counterpointed by the attentiveness which, in every circumstance, however ambiguous and confused, keeps eyes peeled, ears pricked, for the thief's soft footfall.[21]

The sense of final judgment, the sense that moral choices *matter*, and matter absolutely, is one to which our culture finds it very difficult to give appropriate expression. We are at home to horror, but strangers to severity. For the moment, however, my concern is simply to suggest that, in our reading of this final clause of the second article of the Creed, we need to keep in mind that it has application, not only to some distant future, but also to all present thoughts, and words, and deeds.

1. Utterance

One of the few lectures, heard more than thirty years ago, the argument of which is still fresh in my memory, was an exposition by the Irish New Testament scholar John Greehy of a verse from the Fourth Gospel: 'When Pilate heard these words, he brought Jesus out and sat down on the judgement seat.' Who sat down? Pilate or Jesus? Who was judging whom? The grammar is, in Greek, ambiguous.[22] Readers attuned to the irony so characteristic of the Fourth Gospel will appreciate that it is up to them to make a judgment as to who is the judge and, in that judgment, perhaps be judged themselves. This is, after all, not a biography but a Gospel: ' "For judgment I came into this world, that those who do not see may see, and that those who see may become blind." '[23]

Each of the three articles of the Creed says something of the whole of Christian faith, of how all things hang together in relation to the mystery of God. In this section, I shall stay closer to the Fourth Gospel than the other three in the hope that this may make it easier to read this second article as a single declaration or acknowledgment of the single utterance that is God the Word. Nowhere else in the New Testament is the sense so strongly given as in the Fourth Gospel that in this one man everything in heaven and on earth comes sharply into focus, reaches its climax, finds its resolution. God does not, from far away, speak *to* the world. God speaks the world, which finds life in that utterance.

As forms of discourse, creeds, considered in their primary uses, are not all that far from gospels. 'Gospel' is announcement of good news. True, but quite inadequate. *How* do Gospels do what they do? What *kind* of announcement counts as Christian 'gospel'? 'The Gospels are the good news of the risen one told in the form of stories about the earthly life of Jesus.'[24] It does not follow, however, that either the Gospels or this second article of the Creed are biographical in character. In the case of the Creed this is, or should be, obvious: what kind of biography or life-story would it be which mentioned *nothing* that its subject either said or did! In the case of the Gospels, stories are told not primarily to inform, but rather to announce; stories are the form that proclamation takes.

Although neither Creed nor Gospel is biography, the narrative form is, in each case, for two reasons indispensable. It is indispensable, first, because what is confessed, proclaimed, is Jesus. He is not merely messenger, but message. (For now, I merely state the fact. We shall consider, later on, what the message is which is Jesus.) Christianity, I said earlier, is not a 'world-view' or system of beliefs. It is not an ethic or a metaphysic, a theory or an explanation of the world. It is a people with a memory and, for all the world, a hope, both hope and memory finding form and focus in a story with a beginning and an end: the tale of one who 'suffered under Pontius Pilate'.

The mention of Pilate brings me to the second reason why narrative is indispensable for both Creed and Gospel. If Jesus were, like Lear or Prospero, a character in fiction, the truth of Creed or Gospel would depend upon the extent to which the story told of him was 'true to life', gave accurate expression to constant or recurring features of the human drama. This condition the Creed seems not to satisfy at all, whereas the Gospels, for all the strangeness of their world, and notwithstanding their subordination of life-story to

proclamation, do contain much that thus rings true to life (a fact
which helps explain their enduring fascination). Beyond this, however, the Gospels speak of the significance of one who actually lived
and died. Their truth, that is to say, depends in part on the extent to
which they are true to *his* life (and this is the kind of truth we look
for in biography). In other words, the narrative component in
Creed and Gospel is indispensable because both bear reference to
particular past happenings.

However, their primary function is announcement: giving testimony to God's deed or word (John's *'logos'* is still close enough to
Hebrew to carry both connotations). This they do by referring this
one man, and everything that happened to him, to the mystery of
God. They are, therefore, in the last analysis, only true to the extent
that they are also 'true to God'. And that they are so, and may, by
our good use, be made so, is at the heart of Christian believing and
Christian responsibility and Christian prayer.

What the Scriptures say at length, the Creed says briefly. The
second article of the Creed, with its terse catalogue of verbs –
'conceived', 'born', 'suffered', 'died', 'descended', 'rose',
'ascended', 'seated' – sketches a story with a plot. When we read
that article against the background of the Prologue to the Fourth
Gospel, we are reminded that this short story of one man is at the
same time the story of the world – and God. It is a story which begins
in God, beyond creation, 'in the beginning', and which ends in God,
in heaven, 'in the bosom of the Father'.[25]

There have been times and places in which it has appeared, if not
self-evident, at least quite plausible, that all the world and all of
human history might make up a kind of book, a volume which we
can decode and, in so doing, make comprehensive sense of things,
deciphering the world as one vast story with a single plot. However,
all suggestions that the way the world goes is thus 'followable' are,
in our culture, suspect.[26] Knowing how skilled we are at finding what
we want to find, or simply what we put there in the first place, we
suspect that all the stories that we tell are fictions. No, perhaps not
all: bombarded by the fables spun by salesmen and politicians,
knowing how easily we succumb to fantasies that make us 'feel
good', the narratives that we secretly suspect are true are those
which intimate that force, the human face of which is violence, is the

one effective agency in a nightmare of absurd unmeaning. 'Thou whose almighty Word, chaos and darkness heard, and took their flight.' But they did not! If the stories told in the first chapter of Genesis and the Prologue to the Fourth Gospel are found false, then they were falsified not by Darwin, but by Dachau, not by 'science', but by the carelessness which does not even notice the havoc which human beings wreak upon the planet and upon each other as they sleepwalk blindly through the world.

The Prologue does not say, however, that we live in sunshine, but that the darkness has not overcome the light. Despair can be as slovenly and self-indulgent as the optimist's delusions. Our lives are lived from start to finish, from a beginning to an end: we have no option but to inhabit and act out *some* story. What is required of us is that the narratives that we perform, and by the truth of which we take our stand, continually be purified and tested. Maturity, or wisdom, is largely a matter of learning to discriminate.

There is, it would seem, something to be said for, some truth stated by, all well-tested tales. But Christianity (like Judaism and Islam) appears to override such geniality, claiming unique and privileged access to, or purchase on, the truth of things. More shocking still, each in its own way announces that the vast burden of universal truth is somehow borne on the fragile shoulders of one particular people, even (in the case of Christianity and Islam) one man.

On these vast issues, just three brief remarks. In the first place, it is not particularity, in itself, that is the problem. The Christian message is an announcement made in narrative form, a Word that is a history. It is, therefore, less like a theory than a work of art. But it is precisely in particularity that art bears witness to and bodies truth.

It follows, in the second place, I would suggest, that relations between Christianity and other cultural traditions (I avoid the word 'religion', because it begs too many of the questions) should be conducted on the assumption not that they are similar, but that they are different. That way we might learn something from each other. Why should we wish to do so? Not only because the world, a small place getting smaller, is under dangerous threat from human idiocy, but because – in marked contrast to the dominant Promethean secularism – many of the great traditions set high store, each in its own way, on the indispensability of attentiveness, of what I earlier called docility. Each tradition has its own story as to why attentiveness is indispensable (Christians, for example, know that only in a certain stillness may God's utterance be heard), but I see no reason why even vigorous disagreement as to how the world is best interpreted, and fashioned, and its story told, need preclude, in principle, the respectful patience necessary for fostering genuine conversation, promoting mutual education, and furthering common policies to heal the planet's plight.

Finally, a footnote from St Thomas, the orthodoxy of whose doctrine of God's incarnation, God's complete self-gift or utterance in the crucified and risen one, is surely beyond question. His answer to the question as to whether the diversity of things is due to God was: Yes, because no single creature could give God adequate expression.[27] Not even, by implication, God's own humanity, particular flesh. We are thus brought back to the Johannine Prologue, in which the utterance which finds focus in the history of Jesus sounds throughout the heavens and the earth.

We call this man God's utterance, the Word made flesh. Does Jesus' flesh 'contain' God's Word in such a manner that, to hear the message which he is, we should close all other books, block out all other sounds; consider him, alone, in isolation? Or is it true even of *God's* Word that, as heard by us, it takes its meaning from the company it keeps? Where does he *come* from, this strange man 'conceived by the power of the Holy Spirit and born of the Virgin Mary'? From heaven or from earth? Does God's Word thunder from a clear sky, or is it born of long and patient labour?

The answer is, of course, that these are not alternatives. Thus, to begin with, Jesus is – as all human beings are – a product of his society and of its history. To make sense of himself, and of his mission, he read the Scriptures, worshipped in the synagogue. God's Word speaks in Jewish flesh. Jesus is, like every other prophet, sent by God, but it is from Israel that he comes and to Israel (in the first instance) that is he sent. He is marked out from birth, as Jeremiah was, to whom God said: ' "Before I formed you in the womb I knew you, and before you were born I consecrated you, I appointed you a prophet to the nations." '[28]

God's utterance in Jesus, then, the message summarized in the second article of the Apostles' Creed, cannot be heard except in the context of the company that it originally kept: the company of Israel. But, since the message that is uttered there addresses all times and places, languages and cultures, hearing that Word requires the unending labour of its fresh interpretation into other contexts, different situations. There is no time or place, no culture and no circumstance, that does not form part of the company which God's Word keeps. And that is one reason why, whoever we may be, we do not understand it very well.

So far, however, I have emphasized only one side of the story. For the other, we must turn to the Fourth Gospel, which sees Jesus as 'one who had come down to earth from heaven; he would carry out his role as judge while on earth and then return to heaven. John gives no answer to the question *how* Jesus came or how he finally departed.'[29] If anywhere in the New Testament God's Word thunders from a clear sky, it is here, in the Fourth Gospel. And whatever else this powerful vision is, this vision of God's fleshed Word, God's utterance, as messenger or angel sent from God, appearing out of nowhere, it certainly is not history. All attempts to read it as historical description have merely the disastrous effect of transforming it into science fiction.

We need, it seems, to read at least two ways that brief summary of events in the Apostles' Creed: 'conceived', 'born', 'suffered', 'died', 'rose', and so on. According to the first of these, the flesh of Israel speaks God's Word in one whom God then glorifies while, according to the second, the Word in whom God speaks all things descends from heaven, becoming human flesh, and then returns to God. How are these two stories best co-ordinated? A comment on Seamus Heaney's poetry may help: according to one critic, Heaney's work 'gives the double impression that nothing gets lost in the translation of the world into poetry, and that it is only through poetry that the world to which it refers comes fully into existence'.[30] Substitute 'flesh' for 'world', and 'Word' for 'poetry', and we have, perhaps, the clue we need.

The story of God's utterance in the world is, on the one hand, a story of human flesh translated into God's announcement; a story of Israel becoming the 'poem' that is Jesus. Our human flesh becomes God's Word and, in that translation, nothing of our world is lost;

indeed, all things are saved. In every birth, something in a small way similar occurs: the fruit of human labour is a child's cry. But, alone in *that* child's cry, and in its consummation cried from Calvary, there sounds in human flesh the full reality and majesty of God. This version does not, in any way, contradict the other, which gives expression to the prior and fundamental fact that only through the poetry or utterance of God do all things come to be, finding their full form in one man's flesh, in whom we see the splendour of God's utterance.

As seen in him, however, this is a most strange splendour. 'Conceived', 'born', 'suffered', 'died', 'ascended', 'seated': in this sequence, what kind of spendour shines? If this is an outline of God's utterance, what does it announce? What does God's Word *say*? The first thing that we notice is that, although Jesus was a kind of teacher, there is no teaching mentioned in the Creed. This may be taken as a warning not to restrict the sense of 'gospel' to something Jesus *said*. The heart and centre of the gospel is the announcement of the risen one. To make of Jesus a guru or great religious teacher, a master of ethical injunctions, is to lose sight of what the Creed declares. If however, the balance tilts too far the other way, as if what Jesus said and did formed no part of the message Christians proclaim, then Christianity is reduced to a gnostic sect, of no interest save to those initiates who have 'seen' the risen Lord. The first approach forgets that Jesus is the risen *Christ*; the second risks denying that the Christ is *Jesus*.

Perhaps we should say that only in the light of Easter can the history of Jesus be discerned to be the history of God's appearing in the world. With a few exceptions, the New Testament does not speak of what we see, in seeing Jesus, in language that can be construed in triumphal terms.[31] God, we might say, does not appear in Christ as gods and emperors do, with fanfare and retinue and the panoply of power. In the Gospels, God appears as human flourishing: as freedom from oppression, release from captivity, sight for the blind.[32] But *where* exactly, in the Gospels, does God thus appear? Not, it seems, 'in Jesus' so much as in that which Jesus promises, that which his acts of healing presage – as snowdrops in midwinter are harbingers of spring. As we read the story in the Gospels – especially, in Matthew, Mark, and Luke – Jesus seems to be the messenger rather than the message's achievement, God's spokesman rather than God's presence in a transformed world.

There seems to be some knot here which needs unravelling. To help us do so, let me take up again the notion of performative utterance: of words which, instead of describing or evaluating some set of circumstances, do what they say, enact what they announce. The paradigm of such utterance would surely be the creative and redemptive 'Word' of God? God speaks: a world exists, a garden flourishes. God speaks: light shines in darkness, order comes from chaos. God speaks, and prisoners are set free, the wounded healed, the dead are brought to life.

'Conceived', 'born', 'suffered', 'died', 'rose', 'ascended', 'seated': to hear this as God's message is to know that something happens when God says it. To read Jesus Christ as God's Word, God's announcement, God's performative utterance, is to see those things enacted which are, in that utterance, announced. Promising, we saw earlier, is performative. To see what a promise *says*, see what it *does*: in our case (for example) make a binding contract; in God's case, make a world – a people in their place, at peace, with him.

The next step is really quite straightforward, but it is perhaps the most important step of all. If it is in what God's utterance *does* that the sense or content of that utterance appears, then it is in the promised gift, the outbreathed Spirit, that these things happen and, in their happening, we see the point. In other words, the second article of the Creed needs to be read, not only on its own terms, but also from the standpoint of the third. Before doing so, however, there is more to be said of what it is that, in seeing Jesus as the Christ, we 'see'.

I asked earlier: What does God's Word *say*? What, in this utterance that finds flesh as Jesus, does God announce? It begins to seem as if, astonishingly, the correct answer to such questions is: Nothing in particular. Christianity does not provide magical solutions or satisfying explanations, offer us tranquillizers or quick fixes, furnish us with short-cuts past the endless, bewildering and painful labour of making sense of things, of mending our confused and battered world. God's utterance announces nothing in particular: it announces – life! God's message has no specifiable content because what 'appears' in Jesus, what – in the light of Easter – we are made to *see*, is: all there is to see, the whole familiar world, alive. To see that world in him, in other words, is to see it as a place, not of chaos, of unmeaning, arbitrary violence, but as a place of peace, and sense, and friendship. (Before we recoil in revulsion from so strange a description of our bleak and violent world, we should remember that, according to the New Testament, God's fleshed utterance, life's announcement, issues in a cry on Calvary which sounds somewhere between exaltation and despair.)

What, then, does God's Word say? What does the utterance summarized in the second article of the Creed announce? Life. Nothing more, and nothing less. 'And the life was the light of men.'[33] To 'see' Jesus Christ as God's appearance in our world is to see that point. Nothing more, and nothing less. God's light shines in the darkness; shines, not only as the light *in* which we see: the Son sent to illuminate the world – the one 'conceived', 'born', 'suffered', 'died', 'rose', 'ascended' – but also as the light *with* which we see, the *eyesight* that is the gift of God's own self, God's Spirit, to human beings gone blind.

God's shining is the light in which we see, the light with which we see – but only *if* we see. By ending on the note of judgment, this second article, considered on its own, remains (as did the first) ambivalent. That Jesus' story ends in judgment, upon the rest of us, only makes sense if the enactment of God's utterance of life takes place in the flesh of each of us, or fails to do so, and if we bear some responsibility for which way things go. Yet how may human beings properly be charged with working the alchemy that would give the last word, not to chaos, but to order; not to violence, but to peace; not to the darkness, but to light? There is nothing in this article, considered in itself, to indicate how we could plausibly be held responsible for such transformation, or where resources might be found which would enable us, with eyes wide open, unceasingly to work for and announce so comprehensive a healing of the world. If this article is good news, it comes on a somewhat chilling wind: ' "For judgment I came into this world, that those who do not see may see, and that those who see may become blind." '[34]

Lastly, I must moderate a little (but not withdraw) my paradoxical announcement that God's Word says nothing in particular. This is not *quite* right because to put it that way would risk losing sight of the fact that the risen Christ is Jesus: that the form of the announcement of the Spirit's gift is one particular human being who did, and said, and suffered, certain things. God's utterance of life finds focus in one Jew, in whose particularity everything is said. What we might call the 'trajectory' outlined in the second article of the Creed – from conception through Calvary to the throne of God – summarizes our acknowledgment that God's utterance has a *direction*. It has a direction both in the sense that, as given, it directs us, issues a command, and also in the sense that it indicates whither God's gift takes us, maps out the way to life. We could summarize this by saying that the supplementary answer to the question: What does God, in Jesus, say? is: Follow me.

2. Delight

We have already anticipated the theme of this section, the purpose of which is briefly to consider the second article of the Creed from the standpoint of the third. What does God's Word that is Jesus say? As performative utterance, what the Word says is what it does. And what it does is bring all things to life, in God. All good news is delightful. Good news brings delight, or joy, and beauty is what we delight in. It is, accordingly, under the sub-heads of 'joy' and 'beauty' that I shall consider how we hear, in the Spirit, the message that is Jesus Christ. But, first, a further word on judgment.

We saw earlier that God's creatorship, considered in abstraction from the sending of the Son and the giving of the Spirit, is ambivalent. The recognition that all things are created does not, in itself, tell us that they are made, for harmony, from parental love. A similar ambivalence attends this second article, for if God's Word of life speaks judgment, this is not good news unless we know ourselves forgiven, not condemned; unless, that is, this Word is heard by us as 'Yes', not 'No'. Just as it is only in the Son that we know God as 'parent', so it is only in the Spirit that we know God's Word as 'Yes'.

The ascription of such knowledge to the Spirit's gift is not, however, to be interpreted as some gnostic claim to esoteric information. God's gift of sight is not the private property of a secret society. Anyone enabled, in all this dark, to see; anyone with strength and courage, at the dead of night, to keep awake and even sometimes sing (not whistle!), does so in God's Spirit's gift – whatever name they give, if any, to the source of all our patience and our joy.

We can sometimes make some sense of suffering. There is no sense ever to be made of sin. The mystery of sin is the mystery of our ability clear-sightedly to close our eyes, to blind ourselves, to what there is to see: to what is going on, to other people's needs, and so on. When, in desperation, we give up on light, and love, and sense, and beauty, we may pretend that we are overshadowed by some dark god's 'No'. It is, in fact, our own. There is no circumstance that justifies despair (we shall return to this in Chapter VI).

Good news brings delight, brings joy. The news in question is God's Word, God's self-communication, and God is love. Or so we say, but that word 'love' is put, so carelessly, to such variety of use that it is far from clear what 'God is love' might mean. As a guide into this territory, therefore, I shall take Aquinas's account of the relationship between 'delight' and the kind of love that he calls '*caritas*' (not 'charity', a term which has degenerated into the preferred description of those devices by means of which connivance at injustice wears the mask of generosity).

We use the same word, 'love', for avarice and a fondness for ice-cream, for patriotism and an uprush of affection, for the cause of a bereavement's long-drawn pain and for an appreciation of the open air. '*Caritas*', however, is a kind of friendship. Not only does this description exclude, at a stroke, a good part of our loving (it would, says Thomas, with unusual asperity, be ridiculous to speak of being 'friendly' to one's wine) but it takes us straightway to the centre of the Christian mystery. That the unknown God, beyond all worlds, whom we have met as their creator; the Word of judgment we have heard; that this God should be called 'friendly' is the most extraordinary idea. Not only that, but all human friendliness is thereby said to be the finite form, expression in this world, of God – for God is friendship.[35]

Thomas's word for the kind of loving that is behaviour shaped by '*caritas*', or friendship, is '*dilectio*'. God 'delights' creation into life.

To hear God's Word of life, to take God's utterance to heart, is to find all things 'delectable', to delight each other in the light of God. These are awkward manipulations of an English word which no longer suggests anything as serious as friendship. We have confined it to trivial corners of our conversation, as when we thank our hosts for a delightful evening. We do not readily associate delight with pain or patience, resistance to our enemies, unnoticed loyalty or the routines of caring for the aged and infirm. But, though the language may be unfamiliar, the point is not (or not, at any rate, to any reader of the thirteenth chapter of Paul's first letter to the Corinthians), for Thomas goes on to say that all God-given loving, or dilection, or delight, bears fruit, takes effect, in so transforming *everything* we do and suffer that all is done in joy and peace, kindheartedness and generosity.[36]

To take this seriously is to rewrite the script for what will count as virtue for, on this account, no act or course of action – however apparently appropriate or conscientiously performed, however just, courageous, prudent or self-effacing – which quite lacked joy, could, from a Christian standpoint, properly be said to be virtuous at all. Or, to turn it round the other way: to 'believe in Jesus Christ, his only Son, our Lord', *is* so to live out, in his light, all our human lives that their entire performance is suffused with peace and joy and generosity. That this does not make any easy sense (or, if it seems to, tips off the edge of seriousness into pious persiflage) is not, I think, surprising. It is, in my experience, best learned from the kind of radiant tranquillity one sometimes finds in people who have borne far more than most of us suppose that we could ever bear.

To believe in Jesus Christ, his only Son, our Lord, is to hear the message, which is Jesus' story, with delight. But this delight, or joy, which is one aspect of the fundamental form of *caritas*, or friendship, is infectious. There are, apparently, no boundaries to God's delight and hence, by implication, none set to our own. Joy breaks down barriers, seeks company, makes friends.

To believe in Jesus Christ, his only Son, our Lord, is, therefore, to work for community, or friendship, glimpsed beyond all barriers of particular language, culture, class, or race. Which is amazing, and they 'wondered, saying, "Are not all these who are speaking

Galileans? And how is it that ... each of us in his own language ... [hears] them telling ... the mighty works of God?"' As Augustine put it: 'What we observe in the light of truth is what a great and good thing it would be to understand and speak all the languages of all peoples, and so to hear nobody as a foreigner, and to be heard by no one as such either.'[37]

At Pentecost, the crowd's reaction to this irruption of common understanding, of *caritas* transforming foreigners (at least potentially) into friends, was mixed. Some asked what all this meant, but others 'mocking said, "They are filled with new wine"'.[38]

All good news brings delight, or joy, and joyfulness is never entirely lacking in exuberance. Hence, to *hear* God's utterance in Christ, God's 'Amen', or 'Yes', of friendship and forgiveness, is to *see* some celebration, marriage feast, or banquet, even in our present circumstance. 'You shall no more be termed "Forsaken", and your land shall no more be termed "Desolate"; but you shall be called "My delight is in her", and your land "Married"; for the Lord delights in you, and your land shall be married.' What God's Word says is what it does. And what it does is bring all things fruitfully to life, in God, transforming desert into garden, incomprehension into understanding, 'foreignness' into friendship, water into wine. In a nutshell: 'This, the first of his signs, Jesus did at Cana in Galilee, and manifested his glory; and his disciples believed in him.' And notice that, according to the Fourth Gospel, this happened 'on the third day'.[39]

But, great acts take time. The utterance of God's Word of love, engendering delight, is lived as travail: 'You will be sorrowful, but your sorrow will turn into joy. When a woman is in travail she has sorrow, because her hour is come; but when she is delivered of the child, she no longer remembers the anguish, for joy that a child is born into the world. So you have sorrow now, but I will see you again and your hearts will rejoice, and no one will take your joy from you.'[40] To believe in Jesus Christ, his only Son, our Lord, is to bear in mind, in all we do and suffer, the promise of that already given joy.

Good news brings delight, and beauty is what we delight in. Seeing, in the Spirit's gift, Jesus as the Christ, seeing in him God's truth enfleshed as beauty, we delight in God's light enlivening the world.[41] Although, for two thousand years, the wealth of Christian iconography – focussed, especially, in images of mother and child, of crucifixion and of judgment – has borne witness to this recognition in some of the most beautiful artefacts that human beings have made, it is a theme which (especially in modern times) has been surprisingly neglected in theology.[42] This is a vast and fascinating subject, concerning which, however, I shall confine myself to three brief remarks.

In the first place, as I indicated earlier, to see Jesus' story as the shining, in an unfinished world, of God's glory, the appearance – even now – of the beauty that is God, is to set the so-called 'scandal of particularity' in a different light. A work of art is not an instance of a general truth, the operation of a law, but truth shone forth, illumined, bodied, *in* particularity. That one human being should bear so vast a burden of significance is, indeed, quite extraordinary, but our amazement at it is, we might say, astonishment at a scandal of a different order from that of an improbable exception to a general rule.

In the second place, the difficulty that we experience in handling the theme of incarnation as appearance of God's beauty is due, in part, to lack of a 'proper vocabulary to support our ascription of beauty to God'. What, for example, 'would a pretty, handsome, or elegant God be like?'.[43] And any temptation to have recourse to solemn or Romantic epithets such as 'the sublime' is soon cut short by the indignity and violence of the facts which are the form of God's transforming *caritas*, God's healing love. (I have in mind such Crucifixions as the Isenheim altarpiece – commissioned, we should remember, for a hospital – or those of Graham Sutherland and Georges Rouault.) We seem thus to be brought back as the Gospel writers were, to the Isaianic servant songs: 'He had no form or comeliness that we should look at him, and no beauty that we should desire him.'[44]

Christians are familiar with the idea that schooling in discipleship is, in part, a matter of learning to reconstruct the grammar of our ethics: learning to put words like good and just, power and dependence, meekness and fortitude, to difficult and most surprising use. But perhaps such schooling is also a matter of learning to reconstruct the grammar of aesthetics: of finding beauty in unexpected places, unaccustomed forms. Patrick Sherry quotes Augustine and von Balthasar: from the first, 'He hung therefore on the cross deformed, but his deformity is our beauty'; and, from the second, 'we ought never to speak of God's beauty without reference to the form and manner of appearing which he exhibited in salvation-history'.[45] His deformity is our beauty: God works *our* beauty in *his* crucifixion, and, in so doing, 'shows' the beauty that is his. In which, with our eyes opened, we may take delight.

There is, however, one danger with this line of thought, which is that we contract the sense in which beauty is ascribed to God to what we call 'moral' beauty. But this would be to collapse consideration of the beautiful into consideration of the good; aesthetics into ethics. In the third place, therefore, we need to bear in mind that our eyes are opened, not merely to enable us to see Jesus as the Christ, as God's self-shining in the world, but, in his light, to see *all* God's creation as 'appearance' of the One in whom all things are beautifully made. 'To love beauty,' said one Islamic sage, 'is to see eternal life with God's own eyes.'[46] It follows that the ugliness with which increasingly, and often irreversibly, we disfigure the planet – from the wilderness laid waste to the unlovely places in which human beings dwell – is far from being 'merely' an aesthetic failure. Indeed, it is arguable that, from a Christian standpoint, there are no merely aesthetic failures, that 'those who destroy the beauty of creation or who create ugliness may be sinning against the Holy Spirit',[47] God's self-gift in beauty and delight.

A final note, on terminology. In this chapter, I have brought the concept of 'delight' into what may seem, to some readers, to be suspiciously contrived proximity to that of 'light', of God's appearing in the world in Jesus Christ, his only Son, our Lord. After all, as the *Oxford English Dictionary* somewhat snootily points out, only in the sixteenth century did the old word 'delite' (of the same stock as 'delicious' and '*diligere*') get misspelt by 'erroneous' association with such words as 'light' and 'night' and 'flight'. However, words take their meaning from the company they keep and, as far back as about 1236, we find Richard Rolle glossing Psalm 139 as follows: 'That nyght of anguys is made lightnynge til me in my delytis, that is, thorgh crist, that is my delitys, turnand wa in till wele, and nyght til light.'[48]

3. Speaking

'He who believes in me, believes not in me but in him who sent me. And he who sees me sees him who sent me. I have come as light into the world, that whoever believes in me may not remain in darkness.' Although the elaboration in terms of light and seeing is characteristically Johannine, we are here at the heart of the message of all four Gospels.[49] In the case of other embassies, the one sent is not identical with the one who sends (and, if the messenger is incompetent or untrustworthy, the difference can be crucial). In this case alone, the messenger *is* the message sent, the sender's very utterance. Thus, in order to complete the pattern, we need to say something of the way in which everything that Jesus is, and does, and suffers; everything we see and hear in him is to be referred back – without remainder, we might say – to the unknowable, outshining mystery whose utterance or appearance we acknowledge him to be. In this way, we complete our reflections on the second article of the Creed by referring it to the subject of the first.

We call Jesus Christ 'redeemer' of the world. Redemption is a kind of agency, an act, something done. Yet what he did was, in obedience, to undergo his fate. His agency, what he did, is best described as passion, what he underwent. His agency, as messenger of God, is what, in him, God said or uttered: eternal Word once spoken for our life. It is by being uttered that words do what they do: make promises or announcements, heal wounds, pass sentence, speak of love. If we trust someone speaking, we do not nervously keep one ear cocked, listening anxiously to see if we can hear, 'behind' the words they say, some other message which, perhaps, they *really* mean.

Let me run through that again, using not the aural but the visual metaphors. 'He who sees me sees him who sent me.' The Gospel does not say that Jesus Christ is *like* the Father, but, rather, that, in Jesus, God *appears*. The sending of the Son is God's appearing in the world. The one sent, therefore, is God's appearance, God's visibility, the 'face' of God. There is, in God, nothing else to see but Jesus Christ. This is a harder statement to unpack than might, at first sight, seem to be the case. I do not say: there is, in God, nothing else to see but *Jesus*; nothing (that is) but this man as seen by those who see in him only another Jewish teacher. To see this man as God's appearing – 'Jesus Christ, his only Son, our Lord' – is to see his whole story – 'conceived', 'born', 'suffered', 'died', 'ascended', 'seated' – as the fine focus of God's utterance of a world he makes at home in him.

There is, in God, nothing else to see but Jesus Christ. If there were something else to see in God but him, what might it be? Some other 'aspect' of God, perhaps? God may, indeed, have many faces, may appear in many worlds in many different ways. But, to confess Jesus as the Christ, as this confession deepened into recognition of Christ's divinity (as construed after the manner of Nicaea and Chalcedon), is to confess that what is seen, in him, is God's complete appearance. There is nothing missing, nor any point in looking over Jesus' shoulder, for there is nothing more to see.

'The way in which the Son sees the Father is simply by being the Son.'[50] And something similar is true of us, for we have been adopted as his friends or siblings. Moreover, to 'see' Jesus as the Christ, God's Word incarnate, is not to gaze or gape at him, but to see the point: to know oneself called, in absolute dependence upon the mystery of God, to follow him. And, of course, we do so largely in the dark. This is the theme that, in order to round off our discussion of the second article of the Creed, I would now like to consider.

'I have come as light into the world, that whoever believes in me may not *remain* in darkness.' And yet, the darkness still remains. We confess, as Christians, that light dawns, that darkness is not terminal, that – in Christ – resurrection is begun, and yet we need continually to be reminded of the severity of the constraints under which such things are said: under which 'Alleluia' may even now be sung. No one is better placed to teach us these constraints than the Jew. 'To the Christian,' said Martin Buber in 1930, 'the Jew is the incomprehensibly obdurate man, who declines to see what has happened; and to the Jew the Christian is the incomprehensibly daring man, who affirms in an unredeemed world that its redemption has been accomplished.'[51]

Heda Kovaly, a Czech Jew, survived Auschwitz, as did the childhood friend whom she later married. He became a government official who fell foul of the Stalinist regime in Czechoslovakia, was arrested, subjected to a show trial on radio and, on 3 December 1952, executed. This is how she registered her memory of the night before his execution: 'More than thirty years have now passed and that night is still not over. It remains to this day a screen on to which my present life is projected. I measure all my happiness and all my misfortune against it.'[52]

That night is still not over. This is not simply to make the obvious point that the shadow of the Holocaust, and of Stalinism, and of all the other nightmares of our inhumanity for which these serve as paradigm, should have foreclosed for ever the possibility of singing 'Alleluia' carelessly, forgetful of the agony which is the enduring context of all Easter-speech. It is also to insist upon our need, as Christians, to be reminded by the Jew that God's appearing still lies ahead of us, that it is hope, not merely memory; that it is our duty to be schooled in expectation, in attentiveness, through that impenetrable darkness which precedes the dawn. That night is still not over.

What form might such continual discipline, such schooling, take? The question brings us back to the beginning: to the acknowledgment that the fundamental form of all our speech concerning God is as address to God, in prayer. The Creeds are acts of worship. And all prayer, all worship, all human life lived in the discipline of discipleship, is, at its heart and centre, dispossessive. We need continual and exacting schooling because, at every level of behaviour, language, and imagination – from politics to private life, from business to religion – we seek some safety, some security, through ownership and power. And yet, however much we kick against the pricks, we do not *own* the words we say, the things we do, ourselves, our friends, our circumstances (and, when we try to do so, there are always forces, outside our control, which mock all such Promethean ambition). In liturgy and attentive contemplation, praise and prayer, we may learn *to give back* our language, and our understanding, and ourselves; learn patience, the surrender of security, sometimes in darkness not unlike Gethsemane.

'Contemplation,' says Bishop Rowan Williams, 'is a deeper appropriation of the vulnerability of the self in the midst of the language and transactions of the world.'[53] To believe in Jesus Christ, God's only Son, our Lord, is to confess him as God's Word in

human flesh, announcing life. But the *form* of that announcement –
'conceived', 'born', 'suffered', 'died', 'ascended' – was through
appropriation of vulnerability, the Son's obedience, *knowing* the
Father simply by *being* the Son. And something similar is true of us.
We are enabled, in the Spirit's gift, to know our words, ourselves,
all words and all the world, to be secure, in their fragility, as traces
of God's utterance, echoes of the Creator's speech, given back to
God.

VI

Peacemaking

'I believe in the Holy Spirit,
the holy Catholic Church,
the communion of saints,
the forgiveness of sins,
the resurrection of the body,
and the life everlasting. Amen.'

At first sight, this third article of the Creed might seem similar in structure to the second: an element of the threefold baptismal confession of faith elaborated by conjunction with the correspond-ing element from another kind of credal summary. In fact, the differences between the two are more important that any such resemblances. Both components of the second article are con-fessions of 'belief in' God, announcements of the direction in which, we pray, our hearts unswervingly are set. In the third article, in contrast, confession of faith in God the Spirit is followed by mention made of what the thirteenth-century English Franciscan Alexander of Hales called 'four general effects' of the Spirit's work.[1] These other clauses of the article, which thus constitute a partial exception to the rule that the Creed is not a catalogue of items of belief, belong (we might say) to the context rather than the content of our faith in God. Gathering, communion, forgiveness, resurrection: such is the character and destiny of life in God, the Spirit's gift, in whom alone our hearts are set.

'. . . *in the Holy Spirit.*' It is not easy, in our culture, so to rethink what 'creation' means as to render our confession of the world's createdness an acknowledgment of all things' absolute and intimate dependence on the unknown God. Nor are the imaginative frame-works we inhabit hospitable to the suggestion that, in one man's meaning, the whole mystery of God appears. Yet neither task is half as daunting as the effort that is needed – an effort of imagination, I would emphasize, rather than of intellect or erudition – if we are not gravely to misunderstand what is at issue in confessing God as Spirit.

Where would we begin? We talk of 'spirited' behaviour, and of the 'spirit' of an age, but, as applied to God, the latter would sound vaguely pantheistic and it might seem strange to speak of God's vivacity. And yet, such uses do at least retain some sense of *life*, or liveliness. But what of other spirits: gin or genies, hobgoblins or long-dead relations conjured by the ouija board? Do you believe in ghosts? Only in the Holy Ghost. Supposedly sophisticated and well-educated Christians ignore, at their peril, the influence on our imagination of connotations such as these. Words take their meaning from the company they keep and, in our culture, 'ghost' and 'spirit' keep close company with what we now misleadingly call 'supernatural' entities hovering at the twilit margins of our world.

Even more important is the way in which, in its more serious and central uses, 'spirit' takes its meaning from the categories with which it is *contrasted*. Thus, for example, spirit is not-matter, not-body, or not-reason (this last, especially in New Age or charismatic circles), and when bishops are exhorted, or exhort others, to concentrate on 'spiritual' affairs, the implication usually is that these things are loftier than, and different from, such mundane matters as proclaiming good news to the poor and setting at liberty those that are oppressed.[2] At all costs, we are reminded, we must not confuse life in the spirit with politics and economics (advice well calculated to ensure that 'spiritual' preoccupation with psychic self-esteem will leave our economic and political behaviour to grind on in its habitual inhumanity).

Dualisms of body and mind, matter and spirit (the second pair often treated as if, for all practical purposes, interchangeable with the first) now run so deeply and pervasively across the culture that it is easy to suppose them to have been endorsed by Paul, when he distinguishes between the 'physical' or 'natural' body of the first 'Adam' , the 'man of dust' , and the 'life-giving spirit' that is the 'man from heaven' , the new Adam, the risen Christ.[3]

Paul, however, was a Jew, and not a student of Descartes, and his contrast here between two terms which, elsewhere, are often used interchangeably, is drawn between two forms of human life: life as it would have been, bounded by and crumbling in mortality, and the life now offered in the life of Christ.[4]

Throughout both Testaments, at the heart of talk of God as Spirit (and of the world as effect of, and as affected by, the Spirit that is God) the contrast drawn is that between not-life, or lesser life, or life gone wrong, and life: true life, real life, God's life and all creation's life in God. The central metaphor for such life is wind, the breath of God. Whether, sent forth from God, breathing all creatures into being, renewing the earth and filling it with good things; whether whispering gently to Elijah, or making 'the oaks to whirl, and [stripping] the forests bare', or breathing peace on the disciples for the forgiveness of sins; it is one wind, one Spirit, which 'blows where it wills' and we do not know where it comes from nor where it goes.[5] To confess God as Spirit is to acknowledge that the world is not in our control, nor in that of any other creature, system, force, or thing, for everything is breathed by God. To pledge ourselves pliable to God the Spirit may breed anarchy (we shall consider this) but it undoubtedly sets our face against all forms of fatalism.

Finally, lest we confuse the heady sense of immanence – of all things breathed, pulsating, with the life of God – with some form of pantheism, life-force-ism, it is in *Holy* Spirit that we confess our faith. This third article, like the other two, remains an act of worship, recognition of the difference between ourselves and God; acknowledgment, in awe, that every movement of the world towards delight and harmony is played by God as on a kind of instrument, wind instrument.[6] Belief in Holy Spirit, we might say, is dedication to duty in a kind of temple, celebration of a kind of liturgy.

Although the spelling out of the distinction between Word and Spirit – between utterance and the joy that good news brings – as a difference, not merely in our experience of God, but in God's very heart and being, is Christianity's achievement, the seeds were sown in Judaism. What God's Word says is what it does, and what it does is bring all things to life, in God. In the Hebrew Bible, 'What is clear, fixed, and determined about God is his word; the spirit, though her presence is constantly felt, is never seen and never grasped ... like the wind, which in Hebrew is the same word as spirit, she is elusive and impalpable. There could never be any question of her taking flesh.'[7]

'*the Holy Catholic Church*'. God's utterance, I said earlier, announces nothing in particular. What it says and (as performative) enacts is all things brought to life, in God. I later moderated this by adding that the *form* of this announcement, Jesus Christ, is the way to life that we are called to follow.[8] To this, we must now make one more adjustment, for God's self-gift of life does not lack character, or context. And it is the context and the character of God's self-gift, God's vivifying breath, which is indicated in the remaining clauses of the third article of the Apostles' Creed.

Some early baptismal creeds rounded off the threefold confession of faith in Father, Son and Spirit by simply making mention of the church; thus indicating, as it were, the company in which the words we use to speak of God acquire their proper meaning. Having spoken of Jesus Christ, God's only Son, our Lord, said Saint Augustine, we add that we also believe in the Holy Spirit; then holy church is called to mind.[9] It is not, in every case, entirely clear what prompted the gradual inclusion, during the third and fourth centuries, of further clauses specifying different aspects of the Spirit's gift.

We will begin with 'church', a gathering, an assembly, a people summoned, chosen, called together, for some task, some purpose. This people is, of course, the human race: called, *ex nihilo*, into common life, communion, in God. This does not make all human beings Christians. Since the time of Christ, Christians have always been, and seem likely to remain, a minority of the human race. What we usually call 'the church' is that particular people which *thus* narrates, announces, dramatizes, the origin, identity and destiny of humankind. What we call 'the church', in other words, are those who use the language of Scripture and the creeds to proclaim the fact and promise, possibility and requirement, of the 'one-peopleness' of humankind.

But people *are* the language that they use: their gestures, stories, dreams, ambitions; the way they think, arrange, and organize their lives; their rules and customs, memories and fears, criteria of identity and difference, habits of exclusion and of hospitality. The church is a particular people, formed – as every people is – by its particular discourse. But the words and images it uses to render its identity are taken to refer, in principle, to everyone, from the beginning to the end of time. And the history of Christianity is the story of the often terrifying ambiguity of particular identity thus generally construed.

The Second Vatican Council tried to hold the paradox in proper tension by interpreting the church in sacramental terms. The householder in Matthew's parable of the labourers in the vineyard is, according to Gregory the Great, 'our founder ... who has a vineyard, namely, the universal Church, which, from Abel the just to the last of the elect who will be born at the end of time, brings forth saints as a vine puts out young shoots'. It is of this comprehensive fruitfulness, richness of production in the Spirit, that what we call the church is said, in the Constitution *Lumen Gentium* (which quotes Gregory's phrase 'from Abel ... to the last of the elect'), to be 'a kind of sacrament': an enacted and effective sign of union with God and of unity or oneness for the human race.[10]

This church, this gathered people, is called 'catholic', that is: whole and universal. The emphasis, at the time this epithet first appeared in Western creeds, in the late fourth century, was on the catholic, complete, or 'great' church, in contrast to particular, dissident, conventicles and sects. This emphasis thus coloured, without obscuring, an earlier sense of 'catholic', which (from Ignatius of Antioch, in the second century, onwards) affirmed that each particular church, each group of Christians – gathered, in its place, with its 'overseer' or bishop, round one altar – was, in that place, the fullness of the church, the Spirit's temple, sacrament of Christ.[11]

These complementary concerns, with the wholeness of the 'great' church, on the one hand, and, on the other, with the sacramental fullness of what Vatican II called 'all legitimate local congregations [or gatherings] of the faithful', remain, to this day, twin poles which, held in tension, sustain the quest and struggle for the church's catholicity. Each community, suffering and striving and praying in its place, *is* the church of God, the catholic church. But, just because it is the church in its particular place, its very engagement in

the requirements of that place can engender narrowness and paro-
chialism, 'tribal' and sectarian attitudes. It is, in that place, the
church, but what it is required to be, in that particular place, is the
sacrament of 'intimate union with God and of unity for the whole
human race'. Therefore, what we may call the congregationalist
impulse in Christianity stands in need of permanent corrective
pressure from the 'great church' or universalist impulse. Correla-
tively, the distorting tendency to reshape – in structure, theory, and
imagination – the world-wide church after the model of a trans-
national corporation (with corporate headquarters in Rome, perhaps, and branch and district offices dotted round the globe)
requires subverting by the Ignatian recognition that each church,
each gathered group, is the whole or catholic church of Christ.[12]

Finally, we should not forget that, as sacrament of God's creating
Word and Spirit, the catholicity which is signified cannot be
confined to the human race alone. It is the *whole* of God's creation
which finds finishing and healing in the reign of life announced and
celebrated in the wholeness of the church.

Thirdly, this catholic church is 'holy'. This does not primarily or
immediately mean that it is good, or virtuous. Holiness is other-
ness, the unimaginable, unattainable fulfilment of all our hopes and
dreams, perhaps of all our fears. God, alone, is holy, awe-inspiring,
glory-templed. And the purifying touch of holiness can burn.[13] But,
in uttered Word and outbreathed Spirit, the Holy One comes close,
touches and transforms. Holiness is, then, after all, communicable.
Indeed, *all* things are sanctifiable, may be made holy, by the breath
of God. Life in God's Holy Spirit is, accordingly, all things'
existence purified into peace and friendliness, reconciled relationship, sharing – in delight and harmony – in the very life of God.
Hence the enablement, and the requirement, that human beings,
who are moral agents (creatures, that is to say, that bear responsibility for their behaviour), conform their words, and deeds, and
institutions, their treatment of each other and of what we call the
natural world, to the pattern of God's outpoured peacefulness.
Thus it is that, quite properly, but, nonetheless, secondarily and
derivatively, we conceive the church's holiness in moral terms. If it
could be shown that, on the whole, Christianity had made and
makes no significant contribution, by announcement and example,

to the peacefulness and healing and completion of the world, then there would be no reason to give it any further serious consideration. Even allowing for the tendency of those who disapprove of Christianity to exaggerate the damage it has done, there seems no room left for complacency or for triumphalism if the facts of Christian life and history are to be tested by this stern criterion.

'*the communion of saints*'. This clause ('*communio sanctorum*') is perhaps best thought of as an explication of the one before, rather than containing fresh substantive material of its own. It first turned up, apparently, in the resolutions of a synod held at Nîmes in 394. What is less clear is whether it referred, on that occasion, to sharing holy things (*sancta*: that is, the sacraments) or to the shared existence, common life, of holy people. In due course, the latter sense became predominant and thus, eventually, the phrase was taken to refer to the bonds of *caritas*, or friendship, binding all God's people – and, not least, the living to the dead.[14]

In our own day, there are, it seems to me, two good reasons for not losing sight of that early sense of 'holy things'. First, in our struggle to recover a more complete and single sense of what it is to be a human being, an animal that dreams, than has been the fashion since the seventeenth century, it may help to keep in mind that – whatever may be true of angels – *people* can only keep communion, live a common life, through sharing or communion in *things*. Secondly, it is with *all* things – all rocks and stars, all plants and animals – and not only with our fellow humans, that, in the Spirit's gift, we are enabled and required, as constituents of God's one creation, to live in harmony or communion.

'*the forgiveness of sins*'. As the corresponding clause in the Nicene Creed makes clear, this refers first to baptism: 'we acknowledge one baptism for the forgiveness of sins'. From the mid-fourth century onwards, however, its meaning gradually expanded as the recognition deepened that the whole of Christian living – all prayer, all peacemaking, all *caritas* – occurs through the working of God's self-gift, God's Holy Spirit, in reconciliation, the forgiveness of sin. Thus Augustine, preaching on this clause of the Creed, said that since no one lives sinless in this world, forgiveness of sin takes place not only in baptism but also in prayer, especially in the Lord's Prayer, in which we find, 'as it were, [our] daily baptism'. And the prayer over the gifts for the feast of Pentecost in the eighth-century missal known as the Gelasian Sacramentary asks that our minds and hearts may be prepared for the celebration by the Holy Spirit, 'for he is himself the forgiveness of all our sins'.[15]

'the resurrection of the body, and the life everlasting. Amen'. With the affirmation of the resurrection of the body 'the Old Roman Creed reached its climax'.[16] Here, then, the story ends. Which, to some people, may seem surprising. Not only does the Apostles' Creed contain no reference to Jesus' teaching, and make no mention of the eucharist; it says nothing of the immortality of the soul. Instead, it brings us back, we might say, to the beginning: to the completion of creation, in celebration round the throne of God. This may be easier to see if we concentrate attention on the supplementary clause, *'the life everlasting'*.

This clause was added, originally, it seems, in Africa, simply to make it clear that 'resurrection' does not mean coming back to life (like Lazarus, who died again) but being brought alive, in God, with God's own life. 'Everlasting' is, therefore, a somewhat misleading translation of *'aeterna'*. Life, in God, does not go on, and on, and on. It is simply boundless, inexhaustible donation.

It may be understandable that, in our nervous curiosity (for we seem incapable of simply trusting God), we should seek to peer or speculate beyond the boundary of death, to wonder what 'eternal life' is like. Yet all such speculation is, of course, quite futile, for we have, and can have, no idea. But, if we are unable to rest content with Paul's insistence that 'no eye has seen, nor ear heard, nor the heart of man conceived' what God has in store 'for those who love him', we would be wise at least to stay with imagery which, as it were, wears its metaphorical status on its sleeve. Such, for example, is Isaiah's vision, which the Book of Revelation will take up again, of the coronation feast of all creation's king: 'On this mountain the Lord of hosts will make for all peoples a feast of fat things, a feast of wine on the lees, of fat things full of marrow, of wine on the lees well refined. And he will destroy on this mountain the covering that is cast over all peoples, the veil that is spread over all nations. He will swallow up death for ever, and the Lord God will wipe away tears from all faces, and the reproach of his people he will take away from all the earth.'[17]

And yet, the danger of concentrating exclusively on such apocalyptic passages is that we may lose sight of the fact that their purpose is to point us to the *present*, in which we are called upon to pledge ourselves to service in the life of God, the Spirit's gift. As John Colet put it, commenting on Paul's discussion of the 'life-giving spirit' in I Corinthians 15: 'As long as it finds something to give life to, this force of life that makes things good, bright, and alive will press onwards with its vivifying gift.'[18]

1. Donation

The conventional wisdom seems to be that it is more difficult to find words and images appropriate for the 'third' in God than for either of the other two. It would, in fact, seem more accurate to say that there are two ways, irreducibly distinct, not one, in which the impossibility of fitting the mystery of God to frameworks of our imagining is brought home to us. A spatial metaphor may help to put this very simply. On the one hand, God, as creator, as the one by whom all things are made *ex nihilo*, is – as such – absolutely beyond imaginable possibility because too *far* from us, quite outside our range of vision. On the other hand, God, as given life, as intimate to all our inmost thoughts and movements, is – as such – too *near* for us to see. God only comes within our range of vision, is only visible, in Christ; is only audible in the utterance of the Word. It is the one sent whom we see, not the one who sends him, nor the one in whom we see.

Nevertheless, this adjustment leaves untouched the difficulty on which the conventional wisdom puts its finger. It is therefore tempting, in the measure that we can recover a sense of 'spirit' as life-giving breath, 'wild air, world-mothering air',[19] to rest content with such imagery and seek no further precision in the matter. To do this, however, would risk losing sight of the principle that the three there are in God are only to be distinguished from each other in terms of the relationships of origin which they are said to be. God is, indeed, well spoken of as 'spirit', but 'spirit' (unlike 'word' or 'speaker', 'son' or 'father') names no such relationship and is, therefore, not in fact proper to, distinctive of, any one of the three there are in God.

In his quest for a name distinctive of the one whom we call Holy Spirit, Aquinas considers two chief candidates: 'love' and 'gift', '*amor*' and '*donum*'. Following the Augustinian tradition of imagining God as uttering a word and delighting in the utterance, 'love' – as another name for the delight that issues from the utterance – may be taken as distinctive of the Spirit, notwithstanding the fact that 'love' (like 'spirit') may also be appropriately used simply of God's 'nature'; used, that is to say, indifferently of all three in God. And thus, where the overflowing of God's wisdom and goodness, in creation, is concerned, we may say that God's self-gift to all that is not God takes the twofold form of utterance and love.[20]

This seems a small step forward, but it still trades upon an ambiguity similar to that affecting the name 'spirit'. Aquinas therefore tries once more. No one can give what is not theirs to give. To call the Spirit 'gift', therefore, relates gift given to the giver, names a relationship of origin. God gives, and *what* God gives is nothing less than God. 'Gift', then, may be taken as the nearest that we have to a name distinctive of the Spirit of God's love, the gift that is the very 'being-given', or givenness, of God: God as 'donation'.[21]

God, then, is given-ness, donation. And the givenness of God gives life: 'We believe,' as the Nicene Creed puts it, 'in the Holy Spirit, life-giving Lord.'[22] God gives all life, is intimate to every movement, animates all action, fuels freedom, breaks down barriers, breathes dead bones dancing, irrigates the desert making flowers bloom. This line of thought and imagery generates a sense of all things as a single organism, living system pulsating to the heartbeat of the vivifying Spirit. We thus move nearer to the wavelength of the burgeoning recognition, throughout the Western world, that all things hang together, have their place and figure in the rhythms of the dance. Hence the well-known butterfly that flaps its wings in Tokyo, thereby affecting the weather patterns in Topeka, Kansas. And now, this whole delicate and complex web of life is at grave risk, threatened (perhaps terminally) by the arrogance and greed of man. Unless we can, quite quickly, find ways to live within the limits, acknowledging ourselves to be constituents of a larger whole, and not the lords and masters of the world, we shall destroy ourselves and perish in the dying world we kill.

It seems, then, that there are affinities between 'green faith' and the faith confessed in the third article of the Apostles' Creed.[23] Yet many Greens suppose their view of things to run quite counter to mainstream, orthodox, Christian belief. This raises a general issue of importance concerning the relationship between the three articles of the Creed.

These articles do not each deal with some *part* of Christian doctrine – for Father, Son, and Spirit are not 'parts' of God.[24] Each article says something of the single mystery of God and, thereby, says something of the whole of Christian faith, of how all things hang together in relation to God's holy mystery. To concentrate on any one (or two) of them at the expense of due consideration given to the other two (or one) would compromise our recognition of the singleness or simpleness of God, God's oneness. Hence the need to submit the things we say, and think, and do, to continual corrective pressure from the standpoint of whichever other articles or articles do not then form the immediate focus of our attention and concern.

Thus, for example, we confess our faith in God from whom all worlds and systems, light and darkness, pain and pleasure, come *ex nihilo*. We thereby acknowledge that God's silent mystery, beyond all inference and imagination, is quite indecipherable, incomprehensible, unknown. Our hopes and fears alike are, in this silence, silenced. We do not know quite what to make of things. This line of thought, this movement of the mind and heart, is, as we have seen, entirely sound. It is one way that we confess our faith in God. Yet, on its own, without correction from the standpoint of the uttered Word and outbreathed Spirit, it leaves us without good use for the word 'God', thereby encouraging us to set our hearts elsewhere: to worship some fact, idea or thing, some feature of the world (most probably, ourselves). In other words, it generates idolatry.

Or perhaps, we start with faith confessed in uttered Word, in given meaning, in 'traditioned' sense. We inherit rules of speech, systems of value, habits of behaviour. We set great store upon particular places, people, narratives and institutions. We learn to learn, to venerate the message and the messenger: even to confess identity of both in one man worshipped as fleshed Word. This line of thought is (once again) quite sound. And yet, without corrective pressure from the standpoint of the other articles, it once more freezes faith into idolatry, this time by turning God's address, God's truth-giving speech, into our supposed possession, protected by a church now shrunken to a gnostic sect.

In other words, the ceaseless, self-corrective character of good uses of the Creed protects the forms of faith in God from getting stuck: from freezing to idolatry by mistaking some form of our relationship with God for an object of our worship, for God's 'nature', considered as some kind of thing available for our inspection and descriptive mastery. Thus, in the third place, the holistic, immanentist, more or less pantheistic instincts of 'green faith' are, in themselves, quite sound. They give expression to aspects of our faith in God which have been dangerously neglected in modern Western culture. If, however, faith takes this form without corrective pressure from the standpoint of the first and second articles, then we are in danger of freezing faith in God the Spirit into idolatry; at risk either of worshipping an abstract deity called 'Life', or else of worshipping the world.[25]

The Holy Spirit is God's life breathing all things alive, gathering humankind into the fresh peacefulness, finished fruitfulness, of God's creation. The spirit, as everybody knows, gives life; the letter kills.[26] This slogan has often served as banner for the perennially reawakening instinct in Christianity (as in the wider culture), favouring charism over institution, prophecy to priesthood, gospel to law, feeling to argument, heart to head, spontaneity to established custom. Jeremiah announced the making of a new covenant, which God would write, not this time on stone tablets, but on the people's heart.[27] Whether in Judaism or Christianity, the spring-board of 'enthusiasm' is an instinct, not merely of renewal, but of survival: the reaction of the living organism to the threat of suffocation. As Ronald Knox put it: the point of departure of enthusiasm is usually 'a suspicion, not ignobly entertained, that a church in alliance with the world' (with, we might say, the powers that be) 'has unchurched itself', snuffed out the given Spirit.[28]

The antinomian, anarchic impulse within Christianity is thus necessary, not merely for its health, but for its survival. As a corrective, from the standpoint of the Creed's third article, of habits shaped too single-mindedly to requirements (of clarity and definition, for example) associated with the second, what we might call 'the spirituality of spirit' is, therefore, indispensable.

Too often, however, the contrast has been drawn, not between two elements of a whole which flourishes only in ceaseless self-corrective dialectic, but between supposed alternatives. We are then asked to choose: gospel, and not law; prophecy, not priesthood; the inward heart, and not the outward show; to opt for movement, not for institution; not for the letter, but for life. At which point, it is high time to remember that there is, in fact, no such thing as 'life'. There are only living things: flowers and friendships, sea slugs and symphonies, animated conversation and the rhythm of the changing seasons. All life is formed, all living things exist in their particular formation. Form gives identity and shape; intelligibility, character and beauty. And, as is evident across the board – from poetry to pottery, from music to good manners, from athletics to religious rituals, from customs, laws and constitutions – what is true of objects studied in biology is no less true of the elements of human culture.

Form does not give life but, without form, no life exists. Law kills, said Saint Augustine (commenting on II Corinthians 3.6 and, of course, with Torah in mind) when it is only read and neither understood nor implemented: that is what 'the letter' means. And the Spirit brings to life, because the fullness of the law is God's love 'poured out into our hearts through the Holy Spirit, which has been given to us'.[29]

The sense that life flows stronger than the weak defences, seawalls of custom and of institution, which we erect as shelters from the storm, sometimes takes dark, satanic form. Antinomianism may crack and loosen up oppressive structures; but it can also drive the tidal waves of power, the Fascist overriding of diversity and difference, of small-scale, particular existence. In an essay, written in 1924, entitled 'My Universe', Teilhard de Chardin announced that 'There is *only one Evil*=disunity'.[30] But this was the man who welcomed the atomic bomb as evidence of teamwork and co-operation; the man who said, in 1936: 'Fascism opens its arms to the future. Its ambition is to embrace vast wholes in its empire. And in the vigorous organization of which it dreams, it is more anxious than any other system to allow for the preservation of the élite (which means the personal and the Spirit) and to make good use of it . . . Fascism may possibly represent a fairly successful small-scale model of tomorrow's world. It may perhaps be a necessary stage in the course of which men have to learn, as though on a small training-ground, their human role.'[31]

I earlier emphasized the need to unify the world, to gather the scattered fragments of humanity into a common culture, common community, 'the communion of saints' sharing the friendship that is God's Spirit's unifying gift: the peace that binds the body into perfect harmony.[32] But Teilhard's Fascist sympathies remind us that this theme of social unity, this 'third article' motif, is (once again) only appropriately read under corrective pressure from the standpoint of the second: from that reverence for concreteness and particularity which is implicit in our confession of God's utterance focussed as particular incarnate Word.

The oneness, friendship, harmony, created by the Spirit's gift, *requires* and does not threaten or obliterate diversity. It is not difference that is ruled out by God's gathering, but discord; not richness that is incompatible with the Spirit's beauty, but division; not mutual interchange and education requiring (and not inhibiting) disagreement, but exclusion, domination and neglect. Moreover (although this is a theme that we shall consider in a later section) appropriate unity is never the consequence of the violence that we do, the expression of dominative power, but only comes to birth through dispossession. Now, as always, it is through Christ's blood that God makes peace.[33]

At the beginning of this section, I suggested that one reason why we find it difficult to 'put a face' upon God's Spirit, to find appropriate images for the 'being-given' of God, is that, as givenness inmost to every thought and movement of the world and of the human heart, the mystery of God is, as it were, too close for us to picture. Hence the soundness of the instinct that, in our attempts to speak about God's life-giving given life, we should stay close to the biblical imagery of air: God's breathing, all-embracing yet elusive; pervasive, yet in every movement fresh, and unexpected.

This cannot, however, be quite the last word on the matter,

because the life God is and breathes is loving: steadfast affection constituting all creation; affection the human form of which is friendship. God's peacemaking Spirit makes us friends, not only with each other, but with God. Friendship, however, is the very heart of personal existence; it is being friends that makes us persons. Hence the desire to find some way of speaking of the third in God, as of the other two, in personal terms.[34] At least in this sense, then, we need to find some way metaphorically to 'put a face upon' the Spirit. But, when we do so, would it be more appropriate for this face to be given female or male form (these being the only two kinds of faces that we know)?

In the search for correctives to the tendency almost exclusively to use masculine pronouns and images of God, much recent writing has focussed on the third article of the Creed as the place where feminine imagery may most easily and appropriately be used. Two main reasons for this seem to be: first, the association of the Holy Spirit with the feminine figure of wisdom as found in the Old Testament; secondly, the association of the Spirit with the mother-hood of God.

God's wisdom dwells amongst us, gives shade and shelter, makes a home. The wise man, says Ecclesiasticus, 'sets his children in her shade, and camps beneath her branches; he is sheltered by her from the heat, and in her glory he makes his home'.[35] This image is tuned nicely to the sense, in Christian doctrine, of the Spirit as God's indwelling presence, life-giving and refreshing givenness. The New Testament, it is true, tends to associate God's wisdom with Christ rather than the Spirit, but this is on account of the close company kept, in Paul's polemic, between God's wisdom (so unlike that of the Greeks) and his guiding gift of Law which finds, in Christ, fulfilment. Nevertheless, it is only so found, by us, in the measure that, receiving the message which God writes on our hearts, we 'possess the Spirit ... have the mind of Christ'.[36] Wisdom, in other words, remains our teacher.

It is 'in the Spirit' that we learn to hear God's message, recognize our brother, Jesus Christ; in the Spirit that we discover all the world to be the labour of God's fruitful love, learn to relate to the creator of all things as to a parent; and it is the Spirit who educates us into humanness, trains us in the virtues. As in most societies, most teaching in the church is done by women. Motherhood as pedagogy is, it seems, an appropriate metaphor for the Spirit's gift.

Mother earth, mother nature, mother church. Maternal imagery is central to the archetypes of nurturing, personifications of the contexts in which we are, or seek to be, at home. If the church (to use the opening words of an encyclical letter of Pope John XXIII) is '*Mater et Magistra*', mother and teacher, this is both because the church is the appearance, form or sacrament of God's maternal pedagogy, and also because it is, for the most part, women in the church who exercise its teachership or '*magisterium*' (though many of the men still have not noticed this).

Home may be where we wish to be but it is not, for the most part, where we are. In politics, and culture, and philosophy, either the dwellings that we build collapse, or else we transform houses into citadels, fortresses for 'our' security against the 'others', whom we keep outside.[37] Women, like the poor (and, although not all women are powerless or poor, the majority of the poor are women – and children) are often doubly homeless: exiled as all human beings are in an inhospitable and indecipherable world, and excluded from so many of the shelters that men build against the storm.

Rosemary Haughton, therefore, has identified the work of the women's movement as 'part of the great torrent of the prophetic tradition', labouring to make the church 'a place where people [men and women] rediscover the earth as home and accept the work of home-making'. This, she says, is 'the human task of bringing to life. This is what the women of the church are for.'[38] The image of home-making has evident affinities with traditional descriptions of the Spirit as 'indwelling' and 'inhabiting', as making human life God's home, her 'temple'.

We saw earlier how reflection on the first article of the Creed can help us see God's labour as a kind of child-bearing.[39] To this we can now add that images drawing upon women's work in education and in home-making are appropriate metaphors for the life God's Spirit is and gives (with the proviso that the latter set are not so interpreted, in narrowly 'domestic' terms, as to lead us to neglect their wider social and political implications: it is the *world* that God's indwelling makes a home – not simply the suburbs at weekends).

Around the time that the Fourth Gospel found its final form, there appeared one of those early Christian writings which hovered, for a period, on the edge of inclusion in the canon of Scripture: the text known as the *Shepherd of Hermas*. Hermas has a vision of 'an aged lady in glistening raiment, having a book in her hands', whom he takes to be the Sibyl but who is, in fact (the interpreting angel explains to him), the church. She is aged, he is told, because 'she was created before all things ... and for her sake the world was framed'. Much later, his guide says: 'I wish to show thee all the things that the Holy Spirit, which spake with thee in the form of the Church, showed unto thee. For that Spirit is the Son of God.'[40]

The uncertainty with which the distinction between Son and Spirit is drawn should not, in so early a text, astonish us. It would seem to reflect, in part, the fact that (as we have noticed) the Wisdom of the Old Testament may properly be associated, in Christian thought, both with the Word or message that God utters and with the Spirit in whose gift we learn to see, and hear, and do, the things of God. Wisdom has different aspects which may, accordingly, be variously associated with either the Spirit or the Word. Therefore, although the themes of teaching and of home-making may be fruitfully developed in ways that highlight maternal or, more generally, feminine aspects of the mystery of God, neither teaching nor home-making is, in fact, any more distinctive of God's given love, God's Spirit, than 'creatorship' is distinctive of the one in God we name as Father (or as Mother).[41] Wisdom, creator, teacher, home-maker are all good names for God, but none of them names a relationship of origin in God. None, therefore, is, strictly speaking, 'proper' to, distinctive of, any one of the three 'persons' that God is.

Moreover, God's givenness, donation, is no more 'literally' female than is God's Word, or utterance, 'literally' male (as the *Shepherd's* quaint portrayal of the Son in female guise may conveniently remind us). Thus, although there will often be good reasons for using now female, now male images of God – and of *each* of the three 'persons' that God is – we must never lose sight of the fact that *all* gender-specific distinctions belong entirely to the world of creatures, to the '"image and likeness" of a God who, even in his love, is "more dissimilar than similar" (Fourth Lateran Council) to everything created.'[42]

There are two more topics briefly to be considered under this heading of 'donation'. The first, which will serve as preparation for our discussion of forgiveness in VI.3, concerns the mystery of sin, the shadow cast by God's self-giving, and the second voices the suspicion that a gift as great as God is just too heavy a burden for human beings to bear.

Sin is not identical with wickedness. Wickedness is misbehaviour, doing wrong – or failing to do right. Moral discourse has to do with our assessment of the way we treat our fellow creatures and ourselves, whereas to speak of sin is to say something about relationship with God. The contrary of sin, moreover, is not virtue but holiness, conformity to God, being patterned to the character of God whose 'image and likeness' we are made to be.[43]

What, then, is the relationship between holiness and virtue, wickedness and sin? The short answer is that wickedness and virtue are the *forms* of sin and holiness. We mis-take relationship to God in mistreatment of God's creatures. Conversely, we grow in holiness by better treatment of our fellow creatures and ourselves. Since God is not a fact or object in the world, 'sins solely against God are impossible. Every sin is at least against the self.'[44]

To say this is not, by any means, to collapse religion into ethics. The distinction between the two is as absolute and irreducible as the distinction, from which it is derived, between the Creator and the creature. But, just as God is not one amongst the various objects that we encounter in the world, so, too, relationship to God is not one amongst the various relationships that make us who we are. Everything we do and suffer, enact and tolerate and undergo, all the good and all the evil that we do, contribute either to our distance from or our proximity to God, either to sinfulness or holiness.

Moreover, whereas there are many different ways of doing good and evil, of being virtuous or wicked, sin (to speak strictly) is only of one kind. All sin, all mis-relationship with God, is a matter of setting our minds and hearts, our hopes and fears, on something other than the mystery of God; in other words a matter of idolatry. Hence, at the head of the commandments: 'You shall have no other gods before me'; hence Paul's bleak comment: 'they exchanged the truth about God for a lie and worshipped and served the creature rather than the Creator'.[45]

It is in utterance of the Word God is, and in donation of the Gift God is, that all things come to be, and come to be related to the mystery of God. Idolatry, therefore, is rejection of God's message and refusal of God's gift. Since it is this utterance and gift which constitute the creature, sin, as idolatry, is both self-destructive and self-contradictory. It makes no sense. But what is it that, in this mysterious exercise in self-deceptive self-destruction, we suppose preferable to the reality of things, and to the love of their Creator? The answer is: ourselves.

All things exist as expressions of God's knowledge and God's love; as finite refractions of the absolute relations – eternal utterance, inexhaustible donation – that God is. Sin is refusal of relation, self-enclosure in a futile search for safety. There is nothing glamorous or esoteric about sin. Spreading like fungus from dying cities across the surface of the globe, its appearance is only the familiar bleak ugliness of egotism, of the attempt to transform other people, things, facts, institutions, ideas, dreams, into 'our' absolute and indestructible possessions. Karl Marx is out of fashion at the moment, but he accurately identified as idolatrous the alchemy which transforms all creatures into commodities: objects to be bought and sold.

That sin, as refusal of the relations that God is and offers, is self-worship, and that the Midas-touch of egotism turns common into private property, and friendship into servitude or domination, is no new-fangled modern bright idea. According to Augustine, all sin turns 'away from God through pride and self-love, through a preference for private possession over common participation'. And so, in place of givenness, we have only 'gifts', 'donations' from the rich man's table as caricature of God's inexhaustible self-giving. As Edmund Hill's comment on Book XII of Augustine's *Trinity* continues: 'the political and social implications of [Augustine's] doctrine in this respect are really rather revolutionary and subversive'.[46]

From among many questions which this view of things invites, my only interest, at this point, is in the character of sin as antithetical to God's donation, denial of the third article of the Creed. Thus, for example, I am not yet considering whether, and to what extent, our sinfulness is culpable or irreversible. The consideration of

forgiveness will be the proper place to talk of punishment, self-ad-
ministered in the self-destructiveness of sin.

What does need emphasizing now, however, is that mortality,
as such, forms no part of such punishment. God's self-gift is inexhaustible, endlessly creative wellspring breathing life. But, as we
saw earlier, 'life' does not exist; there are only living things, in all
their delicate, astonishing diversity. To confess God as creator of
heaven and of earth is to number death amongst God's creatures,
because the 'earthiness' of mountains, plants and animals (including human animals) is a matter of their limited existence, finite
form. All things start and finish, have a shape, a character, a plot, a
boundary, a beginning and an end; all things are born and all things
die. Finitude, mortality, is inscribed in each particular instance of
God's giving. 'I will die,' says John McDade, 'not because I am a
sinner, but because I am an animal and because dying is what all
animals do.'[47]

Modern Western culture seems driven, as few, if any, other
cultures have been, by 'unbridled, unconfronted fear of death'. This
fear brings with it 'fear of life, and especially a fear of the body'.[48]
Bodies exist only in relationship: bounded and bruised, consumed
and nurtured, battered and befriended, by other bodies. Fear of
death, fear of the body, flight from relationship and responsibility,
daydreams of freedom misread as autonomy attained by the
accumulation of well-guarded private wealth; Promethean mastery
by some minority through controlled violence and ingenious
profligacy; all these are aspects of the flight from finitude which
defines the dark side of our culture. There *is*, these days, a
deadliness to dying, but it is due, at least in part, to the extent to
which 'the human will has malevolently and indelibly inscribed
itself on the world's experience'.[49] But, in the agony of this
confusion, it is still our egotism, self-preoccupation, rejection of
relationship and mutual dependence, resistance to the givenness of
God, which cry out for forgiveness and for healing, not our
finitude.

Meanwhile, each of us is dying. And it is at least worth asking how
we might learn to make of dying acceptance of the Spirit's gift, life
given for the following of Christ. To confess God as Spirit, I said
earlier, is to acknowledge that the world is not in our control. We

do not own the world, nor can we subject it to our mastery. We are simply dangerously gifted aspects of a larger whole. Sin denies such solidarity with each other and with all the world, and seeks alchemically to transmute 'communion' into ownership, gift into private property. Holiness, therefore, takes the form of dispossession, letting go, surrendering the title-deeds we forged.

Life lived in the Spirit is life lived in the following of Christ. Emancipation, letting things and people go from our grasp, is not 'a virtue requested from the Lord on one's retirement'.[50] It is how life in the Spirit is to be lived; which is to say: it is how we are to die. What occurs in death is, in the last resort, the same for all of us: we are deprived of all possessions, 'even of ourselves'.[51] To learn to die (which is, of course, the way that finite creatures learn to live) is, therefore, to learn to relate to each and every person, thing, disease, event, delight, that we encounter, neither as enemy nor as possession but as gift, as friend (notwithstanding Aquinas's strictures against speaking of friendship with one's wine!).

This does not, of course, come easily. It is, says Walter Burghardt, neither 'infused with infant baptism ... nor [does] it arrive automatically at sixty-five'. Indeed, he goes on, the fostering of a climate in which aging could be a discipline of contemplation, a school in which we learned lovingly to attend to things in their particularity and givenness, would require nothing less than a new 'social and economic, political and psychological' climate.[52] Which is not, perhaps, surprising in view of the extent to which our present social practice is structured to denial of the Spirit's gift.

So much (at this point) for sin and holiness. Finally, there is the question as to whether we can bear the gift we have been given. We saw, when considering the first article of the Creed, that the announcement that it is out of nothing that heaven and earth are made is not, in itself, good news. Only as we learn that we ourselves and all things are uttered into harmony do we begin to know the mystery of creation as a bringing of all things to birth in patient or parental love. Similarly, our discussion of the second article showed that God's utterance, God's judgment is not, in itself, good news. It is only in the measure in which we know ourselves and all the world forgiven, enlivened to delight, that God's Word may be heard as 'Yes', God's utterance as 'Amen'. We inferred from these examples that God's 'essential' attributes find their Christian sense only when interpreted in relational or 'personal' terms.[53] If this principle is sound, then it applies also to the third article: to our confession of God as Holy Spirit.

God's utterance lovingly gives life; gives all life, all unfading freshness; gives only life, and peace, and love, and beauty, harmony and joy. And the life God gives is nothing other, nothing less, than God's own self. Life is God, given.

This is our confession in the third article of the Creed. All such celebration is, however, soon interrupted by its sheer implausibility. It seems to fail not only as description of the world that we inhabit and the people that we are, but also as expectation of how things might turn out. Thus, on the one hand, we suspect it may be fashioned from the webs of self-deception which we weave to hide from view, not merely the sheer weight of random violence, isolation, fear, the grinding down of dignity and hope, but (more menacingly to our serenity and self-esteem) the fact that all this desolation has causes: that it is largely brought about, sustained, perpetuated, through structures which we tolerate and illusions which we keep alive. On the other hand, no future that we can imagine could make sense of, let alone explain or justify, the accumulated weight of millennial destructiveness and misery. As Ivan Karamazov said: 'They've put too high a price on harmony.'[54]

All such familiar rehearsals of what is too abstractly characterized as 'the problem of evil' touch only what I called the plausibility of the announcement of God's self-giving love. But, even if, in the company of the Crucified, we find ourselves enabled, without dishonesty or self-indulgence, in some measure to keep faith with God's silence, there is (as we learn from this third article) an even stranger paradox to be confronted.

I said earlier that to believe in Jesus Christ, his only Son, our Lord, is to be bearers, in everything we do and suffer, of God's already given joy; to be pledged in labour to the kind of 'heaven and earth' in which our human work would be the finite form of God's.[55] According to this third article, however, we are so pledged, can be such carriers, because we are even now indwelt, inhabited, inbreathed, by the gift of nothing less than God's life-giving self. Even now, our human loving is the form of God's; our small compassion, faltering courage, most uncertain joy, already breathe God's unconquerable peacemaking power.

We simply are not strong enough for this. To speak of 'guilt' would not go deep enough. Beyond all moralizing, we are, surely, *crushed* beneath the weight of what Ivan's Inquisitor called these 'terrible gifts'?[56] God's gift of life is more than human beings can bear; more than we can carry, more than we can bring to birth. The message of this third article, the announcement that God's life is carried in our hands, sounds most unlike good news.

In this section, following St Thomas, I have taken 'gift', donation, as the nearest that we have to a proper or distinctive name for God's indwelling Spirit, God's presence as creative and redemptive love. According to Augustine, 'There is a difference between calling something a gift [*donum*], and calling it a donation [*donatum*]; it can be a gift even before it is given, but it cannot be called in any way a donation unless it has been given.'[57] But, of course, in addition to these two states of affairs there is the movement or the act of giving. In keeping with my policy of preferring to name the threefold mystery of God in verbal, rather than substantival, terms, it is this active sense of 'donation' that I had uppermost in mind when titling this section.

God's utterance and outbreathing are eternal. The speaking of God's Word, and the engendering of God's delight, are never finished. We should therefore exercise considerable caution in speaking of God's 'donation' in the past tense, as *donatum*. God's giving never leaves God's hands, in which are held all things as ever 'being-given'. In other words, the first step in revision of the dark scenario sketched in the preceding paragraphs is the recognition that God's 'gift', like God's 'utterance', names an eternal relationship of origin. By thus correcting the burdensome impression given, in the abstract, by the doctrine of God's self-gift, we may recover for that doctrine its Christian sense, as gospel.

The Inquisitor, in Dostoevsky's Legend, knows the burden of God's gift, knows the patrician isolation, the rare and dreadful dignity, of this knowledge and its consequence. With a self-importance which seems almost majestically self-denying, he accepts the burden, takes it on himself, to his destruction. When he has finished speaking, however, 'Christ says nothing but kisses the

Grand Inquisitor ... Here, in a single kiss, the most absolute and most appealing part of the Grand Inquisitor's exploit becomes an empty and unnecessary gesture. For him the sacrifice retains its nobility, but the reader sees him as deluded by his ignorance of the dimensions of Christ's mercy ... Christ annuls the romantic acceptance of eternal punishment by refusing to inflict it.'[58] In other words, finding God's gift the dark and indecipherable burden we must bear turns out to be, in fact, just another variant in our endlessly ingenious capacity for egotism, which God's love makes light of.

2. Giving

This section can be brief, because its theme has just been stated. In order for the 'givenness' of God to be good news, and not an imposition too burdensome for us to bear, we need to understand this givenness not as a finished and impersonal fact but as relationship. Our life, as Spirit-breathed, is truly ours, yet still at every moment and in every detail of its being it has its source, it takes its rise, in God. The possibilities that (even in most straitened circumstances) we declare still open, possibilities – such as peace and justice, harmony and friendship – to the achievement of which we set ourselves, are still possibilities of God's inexhaustible and generous fecundity. Thus it is as ever-given by the Father's giving in the Son that God's self-givenness becomes good news, the world's forgiveness, freedom, possibility in God.[59]

We are, in other words, reminded once again that the sense of God arrived at from consideration of any one article of the Apostles' Creed, arrived at (that is) from contemplation of the act and being of any one of the three that we confess as God, requires adjustment or correction from the standpoint of our understanding of the other two. So, in the present case, the sense of God as Spirit, as all things' inmost given life, requires correction both in relation to God as ever-giving, God as 'Father', and (as we shall consider in the next section) to God as ever bearing the burden of this gift, 'the price of harmony', God as Word uttered, Son sent, for our and all things' peace.

The message of each article, considered in the abstract, considered simply in itself, is awe-ful. Who could *thus* 'be-lieve', 'believe in', pledge their minds and hearts and lives and destinies? Against the darkness of existence 'out of nothing', awaiting utterance of final judgement, bearing the burden of this bleak world's possibility, we have (it seems) small cause for celebration. We are, as all things are, dust crumbling to dust (as the Ash Wednesday liturgy and some funeral rites remind us).

The adjustments or corrections which our first reading of each article requires, from the standpoint of the other two, do not, of course, abolish, contradict, or cancel out, the lessons that we learn in fear and trembling. The kind of mindless sentimental drivel, infant's comforter clung to by nervous adults massaging their narcissism, which is often peddled as 'religion' – a kind of drug or pastime helping one 'feel good' – has no warrants whatsoever in either Scripture or the Creed. Learning to read the Creed, learning to treat all thoughts and words and deeds concerning God (and, hence, concerning the constituents of the world that God creates) in fundamentally *relational* terms is, we might say, a matter of discovering terror transformed into wonderment, dread into reverence, alienation into friendship and, therefore, all existence into strange new joy.

Each article of the Creed speaks of the single mystery that we call God, and hence says something of the whole of Christian faith, of how all things hang together in relation to God's holy mystery. What I have tried to show, throughout this book, however, is the way in which each article only yields up its full, its Christian sense when read three ways: first, in relation to the 'person' of whom it makes explicit mention and, then, as modified in relation to the other two. (This is indicated by the structure of this, as of the previous two chapters.) But, of course, this principle also operates among the articles – requiring each one to be read, and reread, in relation to the others. Only when read in some such way as this does the Creed function, effectively, as a Christian pattern of belief: both positively, as guidance for, and negatively, as self-correction or restraint upon, our uses and misuses of the names of God.

I said earlier that faith in God as immanent, as given Spirit, presence pervasive of all life and possibility, risks freezing into either worship of an abstract deity called 'life', or else of worship of the world. World-worship may, of course, take many forms, but few run deeper, exercise a more plausible and powerful hold upon imagination and behaviour, than the worship of necessity.

By worship of necessity, I do not mean the mere acknowledgment that the possibilities open to us – whether as individuals or as social groups of varying complexity and influence: as movements and associations, corporations, nation-states, cultures and religions; or simply as the human race – are, in fact, exceedingly restricted. The planet has been brought, in large part by human energy and greed and ingenuity, to a point at which vast networks of production, distribution and exchange, masters (increasingly) not servants of the processes of politics, in principle uncaring of their cost in poverty, mistrust and violence violently contained, squander non-renewable resources, daily destroy whole species, and now threaten the survival of our lands, our seas and of the very envelope we breathe. To acknowledge that this is the situation, and that there is little that can be easily or painlessly or rapidly be done about it, is not idolatry but realism.

By worship of necessity, I mean so focussing on these limits of our human life, on these constraints to our existence, as to render *absolute* our impotence, our victimhood to forces and to structures outside our control, our slavery to some malign taskmaster – fate, 'the market', call it what we will – at whose throne we kneel. Another name for worship of necessity, therefore, is despair.

There are (to simplify) three common counter-strategies to such fatalism, all of which are doomed to fail because, in one way or another, they accept, perhaps unwittingly, the premises from which despair proceeds. First: if we now are slaves, then we may hope one day to be masters. So turns the treadmill of the struggle for dominance – between individuals, between human groups, and between human beings and the 'natural' world of which they form a part. We can now see, more clearly than our predecessors could, the outcome of this struggle in our destruction of, and by, a dying planet.

Secondly, if we now are slaves, we can (perhaps) hope one day to be free. But, when freedom is construed as 'my' (or 'our') posses-sion and control of space, of things, of actions, then we are still stuck upon the treadmill. Still worshipping necessity, we seek to snatch its fire, and struggle to be little masters, little gods. Thirdly, we can surrender all the 'outer' world – of facts and bodies, birth and death, of structures, laws and institutions – to the inexorable revolutions of the wheel of fate, while yet attempting to carve out private 'inner' spaces in which to find, at least in our imagination, some shelter from the storm.

None of these three strategies seriously challenges or calls in question what I called the premises from which despair proceeds. Each, in its own way, acknowledges the bleak, unsmiling, valueless and ineluctably all-mastering processes and structures, laws and forces, which, ultimately, absolutely (it is said) constitute the 'real' world. Each of these strategies is, therefore, better thought of as a deviant by-product of, or variant upon, the worship of necessity than as its refusal.

That all events and institutions, things and people, forces and processes within the world, are just brute facts, expressions of imperious necessity, is not itself a further fact about the world. It is one way of telling a most sophisticated story: a story which, while not self-evidently true, is not, by any means, self-evidently false. We learn such stories, and discern their truth or adequacy, by being participants in cultural contexts which entertain them and, perhaps, endorse them, embodying them in social practices. All forms of worship, all structures of belief, require such 'schools', such contexts of transmission and sustained identity.

Cultures are no more impermeable than natural languages. In either case, there are degrees of being 'at home', and, at least where what we might call 'partial' cultures, particular territories of discourse and behaviour are concerned, it is not necessarily more difficult, in principle, to inhabit several climates of belief than it is to be at home in several languages. Most of us manage it, without undue strain, most of the time. Nevertheless, conflicts and contradictions do arise, requiring us, from time to time, to choose one narrative, one system of description, one frame of reference, rather than another. And, of course, the more comprehensive the range or scope of the conflicting narratives, the heavier with consequence the choice we make.

To speak of 'choosing', here, however, may be misleading. If the word conjures up images of people with full purses wandering round well-stocked shelves, casually selecting a basket of commodities, then it could hardly be more inappropriate as a description of the *labour* that we call 'conversion'. Yet this was the kind of choice, or fundamental option, that I had in mind: 'I have set before you life and death, blessing and curse; therefore choose life, that you and your descendants may live, loving the Lord your God, obeying his voice, and cleaving to him.'[60] What would such choice *look like*? What kind of transformation would such choice entail?

Imagine (for the sake of illustration) that we inhabited a culture which set the highest store by individual space and rights, autonomy and freedom – there is, as Margaret Thatcher said, 'no such thing as society'; a culture which, rendering all relationships subordinate to individual preference and pleasure, knew little of disinterested duty or enduring loyalty; one which, moreover, saw human wealth, or flourishing, in terms of ever-larger piles of things, arranged in ever-wider well-fenced spaces (all things and spaces being someone's 'private' property).

From such a world, consider just how vast a work of reconstruction would be necessary, how comprehensive a reshaping of head and heart and habit, of narrative and social institution, if its inhabitants, though with eyes wide open to all the danger and the savagery of the world, were truthfully to tell its story, and their own, as (in the last analysis) a story not of fate or blind necessity, of individuals struggling for survival in a lottery, but – from start to finish, from the world's beginning to its end – as the story of the creation of a place of tranquil friendship, of the giving and receiving, quite gratuitously, of good gifts.

Yet this, it seems, is just what is entailed by our declaration, in the Creed, that God is Holy Spirit. God, we say, proceeds from God 'by way of love', as inexhaustible donation.[61] God's self-presence, constitutively intimate to every creature, is pure giving, boundless generosity, healing of all things by its breathing into peace. To 'believe in' God, life-giving Holy Spirit, is to be dedicated to the labour of such generosity's appearance.

According to one ancient and influential story of the world, all things begin from violence and proceed, through endless conflict and sometimes heroic struggle, to exhaustion on a corpse-strewn battlefield. Christianity, however, tells another tale, according to which in the beginning, and the end, is peace, pure infinitely being-given peacefulness which, in the times between, makes its appearance in the endless uphill labour of transfigurative harmony.[62]

The school, or culture, which we call 'the holy Catholic Church' exists, in other words, to serve as sign or sacrament of God's self-giving, performative announcement of the Spirit's gift. Nowhere does the mystery of sin cast darker shadows, therefore, than when this 'communion of saints', assembly of holy people sharing holy things, complicit in the cult of private property, reinforces just those structures of domination, enmity, death-dealing, which blot out from the world the Spirit's radiance, exacting – as the price of harmony, the form of our forgiveness – blood spilt by God's own flesh.

3. *Forgiving*

God does not leave us to our own devices, burdened by responsibility too great for us to bear. God does not give commands we are unable to fulfil, or talents which we lack the skill to put to fruitful use. God's gift is nothing other than the strength of God's own friendship, the constancy of God's self-giving, breathing all the world alive. But, though this recognition renders the doctrine of God's gift good news, it does not, in itself, release the captives, give sight to the blind, or set at liberty those who are oppressed.[63]

Ivan Karamazov's question stands: 'What have the children to do with it?' No future that we can imagine, no distant vision or utopian fantasy, could justify the suffering of the innocent or yield the promise of a happy ending that would permit us to forget their pain. It turns out, however, that justifying and forgetting do not exhaust the possibilities. Between them lies the mystery of the world's redemption, the mystery of God's for-giving. In this final section, therefore, we shall explore the 'second article' correction to our exposition of the doctrine of God's Spirit, to the effect that, in the dying of the Son, it is God's own self that bears the burden of God's giving in a world of sin and evil and, through this blood shed, brings all things alive in peace.

   The roll-call of metaphors clustering round the mystery of sin and its forgiveness, metaphors drawn from law and medicine and commerce, justification and salvation, redemption and atonement, bears witness to the extent to which modern Western theology, and especially its Protestant Augustinian versions, so focussed attention in this area as dangerously to neglect the doctrines of creation and the Spirit's gift. It seems inevitable, therefore, that the re-integration of our Christian understanding within the trinitarian pattern and rhythms of the Creed will call for some reworking of these metaphors.

   God does one work, which is the finished world. God makes this world *ex nihilo*. There is no raw material, no stuff resistant to the craftsman's touch, nothing (we might say) that could make God sweat or labour. And so (in Chapter IV, 1) I incautiously inferred that, if God makes the world *ex nihilo*, he makes it without effort. However, we saw in the very next section that this will not do. There is, indeed, nothing 'outside' God which could constrain God's act, frustrate its purposes. And yet God's deed, it seems, is not uncostly. The Almighty One does labour, does bring forth maternally, that fruit of love which is the finished world, alive.

   There is no natural force constraining God. If, therefore, there is that which makes God's utterance costly, requiring – as the price of harmony – that God's own flesh should bleed, then this must surely be some almost godlike agency, some most impressive, dark and awe-inspiring power? The pressure to think in this direction, imagining chaos to be an entity competitive with God, or personifying evil in the form of Satan, is, and has always proved itself to be, extremely strong.

   And yet, all such temptation is to be resisted. If the peace made by the blood of him in whom all things were made, the peace that is the Spirit's gift, is itself forgiveness of sin,[64] then the mysterious dark power which God's love conquers turns out to be nothing more magnificent than our capacity for madness: our ability – for a little while, at least, but with appalling consequences – to say 'No' to God. Before we take things any further, therefore, it now seems necessary to spell out a little further just what we mean by 'sin'.

   Sin, I said earlier, is not the same as wickedness. Nor, I would now add, is sin the same as evil, if only for the reason that we speak of physical as well as moral evil: of suffering and disaster undergone in circumstances in which it simply makes no sense to talk of praise or blame, rewards and punishments, guilt or responsibility. (We would, for instance, be mistaken if we were to 'blame' Mount Etna for destroying villages with molten lava, and the villagers, in turn, would be mistaken if they interpreted their tragedy as punishment for sin.)

Sin, wickedness, and evil. These three concepts, I suggest, describe malfunctionings in God's creation, states of affairs concerning which our Christian faith in the Creator entitles us to say: 'This is not the way things ought to be.' 'Evil' names the widest circle of the three, and 'sin' the narrowest. All sin and wickedness are evil, but not all evil that befalls us is attributable to either wickedness or sin, and not all wickedness is sinful. Sin makes no sense at all, and wickedness makes not much more. In fact, *all* evil stands at or beyond the edge of understanding.

Consider, for example, just how paradoxical it is to speak of God's creation as malfunctioning. Creation is the world God makes, from nothing, out of love. And love's almightiness makes all things well. And yet, even when due allowance has been made, first, for our propensity to sentimentalize the randomness of evolution and the violence that is, in part, constitutive of natural processes – from earthquakes to the world of living creatures, and, secondly, for our apparent inability to rest content with finitude, there are still aspects of the way things are against which we protest that this is *not* the way things ought to be. Thus, even before we mention wickedness and sin, there is a 'travail' that we do not understand – what Paul calls 'bondage to decay' – in the apparently unending labour of love's almighty ordering of all things into peace.[65] Alone (so far as we can tell) amongst the kinds of things there are, human beings experience 'the price of harmony' as restlessness or yearning, protest or contemplative *complaint*, and, by the same token, as the capacity, in the Spirit's gift, and the requirement, in the following of Christ, to contribute to the making of God's finished peace. Which capacity we regularly squander; which requirement we habitually fail to meet.

Failure, of course, is widespread in the world: it is a function of the processes of evolution. Crops fail, and populations; individuals and species fade away and die. But in human beings alone are failure and what I have more generally called malfunctioning transformed into *moral* issues. Alone amongst God's creatures, human beings have duties and responsibilities, the gift of free relationship. Only human beings, therefore, are capable of holiness and virtue, wickedness and sin.

The textbooks used quite confidently to distinguish between 'material' and 'formal' sin: between wrongdoing and wrongdoing freely undertaken in the knowledge that it was, as wrongdoing, against the will of God. My distinction between wickedness and sin requires us to put the matter somewhat differently. *All* mistreatment of God's creatures is both materially wicked and materially sinful. But only mistreatment that is freely done, and done in the knowledge that it *is* mistreatment, is formally wicked (and therefore culpable). And only the formal wickedness of those who recognize mistreatment of the creature to be mis-relationship with God is also formal sin.

It would seem to follow that what we might call the sinfulness of sin varies in direct proportion to recognition of the boundless generosity, inexhaustible forgiveness, of the love of God. 'Father, forgive them, for they know not what they do.'[66] Does it follow that clear-sighted sinfulness is unforgiveable, impermeable even to God's transforming Spirit, or that 'pure' sin, absolute refusal of relationship with God, is beyond even our capacity for destructive lunacy? We shall return to this.

The world is still unfinished; its history has still some way to go. And there has never been a time, it seems, when all things have been exactly as, according to the Creed, they ought to be. In some sense, then, evil is as old as time. But wickedness is very recent; so is sin – for human beings have not been around for very long. And, even after human malice and stupidity had begun to wreak their havoc, it was not, for many centuries, all that difficult (in principle) to distinguish between 'natural' disasters and the consequence of sin. Now, as the system or structure of the world becomes, increasingly, one complex fact – culturally, politically, technically and economically –, one large *artefact*, one single outcome of human energy and ingenuity, the stain of our malevolence has spread across the surface of the globe. Pollution of the air and seas, deforestation and expansion of the deserts' range, annihilation of innumerable species and exhaustion of non-renewable resources – all these and similar phenomena are caused by human arrogance, short-sightedness and greed. Famine and mass starvation, these days, are no more 'natural' disasters than are deaths caused by the collapse of a building which the landlord neglected to repair. They are consequences, albeit in some measure unforeseen and un-intended, of human action and inaction, of someone's wickedness or sin.

The three concentric circles of non-moral evil, wickedness and sin are rapidly becoming coextensive as the plague of human folly tightens its grip, threatening the planet and the human race with violent, premature, slow death. One thing, at least, seems obvious: that the world's redemption is quite beyond our human capacity. I have (I must admit) more sympathy with those who say that there simply is no forgiveness strong enough to heal this darkness into daylight than with those who cheerfully insist that things are really not that bad after all. There does, at least, seem fresh scope for plausibility in the Christian doctrine that nothing less than God's own suffering is required to bring this world to birth in peace.

Before we move on to consider God's work of forgiveness, there is one more question to be asked concerning sin. Are there different kinds of sin? I suggested earlier that, strictly speaking, there are not, and that sin is only of one kind. And yet it used to be the custom, in Catholic theology, to speak about three kinds of sin: mortal, venial and original. Recently, it has become the fashion to talk not of 'mortal' but of 'grave' or 'serious' sin.[67] This seems to me a most unfortunate development, inasmuch as it implies that there could be such a thing as 'trivial' sin, or sin that really did not matter very much at all.

But sin is self-destruction, refusal of God's creature-constituting love, chaos-engendering idolatrous self-absorption. *All* sin is mortal, deadly, terminal disease. All sin snuffs out the breath of God, extinguishes the Spirit. I am suggesting, then, that we should take the primary and focal sense of sin to be what once was known as mortal sin, thereby acknowledging that other uses of the word are metaphorical, derivative. It would then follow that, grammati-cally, the relationship between (mortal) sin, venial sin and original sin is more like that between catch (as in catch a ball) and catch (as in catch on or understand) than like that between apples and oranges, which are two kinds of fruit.

All of us are sinners, not in the sense that each and every one of us is, already, self-destroyed (or damned) but in the sense that we are all diseased, our friendship with each other and our love of God occluded, weakened and confused, by the sin-infected character and structure of our circumstances, at which incipient deadliness we each – by selfishness, and cowardice, and carelessness – connive. In the unending struggle, within each of us, between holiness and sin, it is this connivance, this tawdry and pervasive feebleness in all our friendship, this dissipating listlessness before the face of God which we once called 'venial sin' (a usage about as helpful as it would be to call discourtesy 'venial murder').

There is a sense, then, in which all of us are sinners, and it seems as though this is the way that things have ever been, from the beginning, *ab origine*. Ever since our species' first emergence in the world, we have proved adept at self-worship, violence and betrayal. Moreover, just as friendship, fostered and sustained, ripens into cultures of relationship, institutions of the Spirit's gift, so also cowardice and greed congeal into practices and systems of destructiveness and inhumanity. (Not that these two types of institution are, empirically, ever quite distinct: wheat and weeds grow, inextricably intertwined, until the harvest.) Nor does there seem good reason to suppose that God's forgiveness, laborious donation of the Spirit of the Crucified through human hearts and practices, will ever finally transform, definitively overcome, our strenuous resistance to reality before the finishing of Paradise, the end of time, the 'appearance' of the Lamb whose coming 'takes away the sin of the world'.[68] Thus, the forgiveness of 'original' sin is, as we would expect, the finishing of God's creation.

Sin makes no sense, and therefore its forgiveness is difficult to understand. The most important thing that we can do, in our attempts to make some sense of things, is to ensure that all the concepts and the images we use point us towards, and do not distract us from, the *oneness* of the mystery that we confess as Father, Son and Holy Spirit.

We can begin by noticing how questionable is Ivan Karamazov's image of suffering as the 'price' of harmony. Who sets that price and, having set it, stands aside, demanding payment? The only answer possible, it seems, is God. But this is not the God confessed as absolute self-gift, as being himself 'forgiveness of all our sins'.[69] And this forgiveness which God's gift is is exercised, enacted, undergone, in God's own utterance, God's fleshed Word's last cry.

Too many images or interpretations of the mystery of our redemption make one or both of two mistakes. *Either* the Son is separated from the Father – as in accounts of God 'demanding' Christ's blood shed, Moloch requiring human sacrifice, *or* what once was done by Christ on Calvary is disconnected from the things which, in the Spirit, we are now enabled and required to do.

All versions of the first mistake infringe the principle that the three there are in God are only to be distinguished from each other in terms of the relationships of origin which they are said to be. God's pure parenthood bears fruit, against the grain of sin and evil, through the unswerving trust and faithfulness of him who, even at the heart of darkness, knows himself thus born.[70]

Mark's Gospel says that Jesus, in Gethsemane, 'began to be greatly distressed and troubled'. Began to be: Jesus' terror deepens as he goes to Calvary. (Of what was Jesus frightened? Not, surely, simply of the death that he saw coming?) There, when darkness had covered all the land, he called on God, who seemed to have abandoned him, then someone filled 'a sponge full of vinegar, put it on a reed and gave it to him to drink'. That mention of vinegar is a kind of footnote, referring us to Psalm 69: 'Insults have broken my heart, so that I am in despair ... They gave me poison for food, and for my thirst they gave me vinegar to drink.' A little earlier, the psalmist prays: 'At an acceptable time, O Lord, in the abundance of thy steadfast love answer me. With thy faithful help, rescue me from sinking into the mire ... Let not the flood sweep over me, or the deep swallow me up.'[71]

It is as if God's own utterance, which makes the world, *itself* is threatened by the chaos-waters which, 'in the beginning', by that Word are set in place, and which, by that same Word, were parted at the sea of reeds to let God's people pass to life and freedom. I would not be wandering too far from Mark's text if I suggested that what occurs on Calvary in the death of Christ is that which happened 'in the beginning' and at the Exodus: God's Word makes a world, a home for us with him.

The spring festival, rather than mid-winter, once marked New Year's Day. On 25 March, according to the fifth-century calendar known as the martyrology of Jerome, 'Our Lord Jesus Christ was crucified, and conceived, and the world was made.'[72] On this day God brings all things alive, *ex nihilo*. Out of nothing, by his word, he makes a world, a home. Out of the virgin's womb, Christ is conceived. Out of that world-threatening death on Calvary, life is new-born from an empty tomb. Christ's terror is God's Word's human vulnerability. But, it is just this vulnerability, this surrender, absolute relationship, which draws out of darkness finished life, forgiveness of sin.

The second mistake that is often made in interpreting the mystery of our redemption consists in separating what was once done by Christ on Calvary from the things which, in the Spirit, we are now enabled and required to do. Amongst the ways in which this happens, I will mention two. In the first place, there are accounts which would reduce God's work in Christ to the setting of an example for the rest of us to follow. But, even if we learn, from Jesus' life and suffering, and the manner of his death, something of how we might appropriately live, forgive, be reconciled, as human beings, the mere establishment of an ideal does not change the world, transform society, uproot the darkness and destructiveness of sin, strengthen us into gentleness and peace. According to this story, God, in Christ, does not forgive our sin, but only sets us an example that we cannot follow, thereby deepening, by contrast, the darkness in which we still seem stuck.

In the second place, there are accounts which speak of Jesus' violent death as the inevitable outcome of the clash between God's love and human wickedness. In some versions of this story, it seems that those who killed him, those who engineered his execution, were thereby unwitting agents of God's love, collaborators in a kind of cultic sacrifice or ritual murder which, *as such*, achieved the reconciliation or forgiveness of the world.

Neither of these readings of the life and death of Christ is simply false. What God says and does in Christ does furnish an example (which is one reason why Christian living is a matter of the following of Christ) and, as we have seen from several different points of view, the mystery of sin and evil renders loving, even God's loving – which is unbounded giving, and forgiving and life-giving – laborious (using that word, once again, to indicate the tragic dimension to the history of the world).

Where both these readings miss the mark, however, is in their attempt to see the work of our redemption displayed in Jesus' life and death considered in isolation from the Spirit's work: in abstraction from 'the holy Catholic Church, the communion of saints'. In other words, they lose sight of the performative character of God's utterance. What is said, in Christ, is what is done in the Spirit: the practice of forgiveness in the polity, and institutions, and relationships, that we call 'church' (and that ceases fully to be church in the measure that these things are not done there).[73] Where does God's forgiveness occur? In our transformed behaviour as the outcome, in the Spirit, of God's utterance in the life and death of Christ.

It is God's own self that bears, on Calvary, the burden of God's giving and, through this blood shed, brings all things alive in peace. *All* things. When the psalmist prays that the king may be endowed with God's own 'righteousness' and 'justice' (concepts both of which have played a major part in Christian doctrines of redemption), the range of blessings compassed by these attributes runs far beyond the moral sphere, the territory of wickedness and virtue, to peace, prosperity, and fruitfulness for both God's people and the land.[74]

We are thereby brought back, in the end, to the beginning, for the world's forgiveness is creation's finishing, and to confess our faith in God as Holy Spirit (who 'is himself the forgiveness of all our sins') is to pledge ourselves in service to the labour of what might be called the politics and ecology of the world's peacemaking. Moreover, as disciples of the Crucified, we do so with our eyes open, under no illusion that death and mourning, crying and pain, have yet passed away.[75]

But, pass away they will, or creation would remain unfinished, God's utterance interrupted, peacemaking incomplete. Life is God, given, and 'life everlasting' is the fruition and fulfilment of life's gift, in God. Even amongst Christians, there are some who say that heaven is too much to hope for, and that we now have hell enough to have no fear of it hereafter. On heaven, I have two things to say, but only one on hell.

In the end, God heals absolutely, makes all things new. We do not understand this because, as I said earlier, no future that we can imagine could justify injustice, make sense of innocent suffering, or yield an ending that would permit us to forget the children's pain. But what, I think, needs emphasizing is that to 'believe in God' after the pattern of the Creed is, nevertheless, to hope for nothing less than this, to hope for nothing less than everything. It is not as though we could excise the last two clauses of the Creed's third article and still stand by the rest. To believe in God as Father, Son and Spirit, is to believe that nothing less than God is given, for our life. And this is heaven.

That is the first thing that we need to say. And the second is that this is *all* that we can say. In the end, God heals absolutely, but we work in the meantime. And we have better things to do than speculate about the future. Concerning the details of the outcome of the world, in God, we have no information now that Jesus lacked in Gethsemane. What we have been given, in the Spirit, is the ability to work, and sing, and suffer, in the knowledge – learned from what is said by Calvary and Easter – that all will one day be well.

And yet, this bright hope is darkened by the shadow of our egotism, the Midas-touch transmuting everyone and everything into either private property or potential threat, either consumer or commodity consumed. Is it possible that groups, and individuals, can so consistently twist tight the screw of self-obsession, of self-worship, as to become impregnable to God's transforming generosity? Are human beings able to enact so resolute a 'No' as self-destructively to contradict God's life-giving 'Yes', heaven-constitutive 'Amen'? We do not know, but to exclude the possibility would seem too easily to set aside the evidence of destructive arrogance and cruelty which makes our world, throughout its history, a kind of Golgotha, or place of skulls.[76]

VII

Gardening

What the Scriptures say at length, the Creed says briefly. But the Scriptures speak of all things in relation to the mystery of God. There is nothing, therefore, of which the Creed does not, albeit briefly, speak. It declares where all things come from, and where and how they go, from the beginning to the end, from Alpha to Omega. In the beginning, God created the heavens and the earth and, in the end, the one who sat upon the throne said: 'It is done.'[1] Great acts take time, and time is what God's peacemaking utterance takes.

'The Lord God planted a garden in Eden, in the east,' in the direction of the rising sun.[2] We can read the Scriptures as the story of this garden made by God in which his people dwell at peace with him. There are three ways in which the tale is told, ways which (without too firmly pressing the suggestion) may be taken to correspond to the three articles of the Creed.

Thus, in the beginning, the story of the world is told as God is producing it, as it ought to be but, as yet, is not: God's garden.[3] Then, in the end, the story of the world is told as it will be, when God's peacemaking is complete: as paradise with 'the tree of life with its twelve kinds of fruit, yielding its fruit each month; and the leaves of the tree were for the healing of the nations'.[4] And, in between, there is another story of the garden as a place of sweat, and blood, and pleading, and betrayal; a place of darkness, of the night, which is, however, also a place of most mysterious appearance, a place of freshness and unexpected recognition. This is the story of the time between and of the way in which the wilderness is made to be what it both should and will be: paradise, God's garden.[5]

Noah, according to one strand in the book of Genesis, was the world's first gardener, 'first tiller of the soil. He planted a vineyard.' But, of course, he could not do so until the flood-waters of chaos and destruction had been held back, allowing dry land to appear. This happened on the first day of the month of Nisan, New Year's Day, the day on which Yahweh's first temple, 'the tabernacle of the tent of meeting', was constructed in the desert. Chaos is not, by any means, a merely 'natural' force or threat. It also has its human form, as wickedness, in enmity and violence. Therefore, through Moses' agency, God holds the waters back, letting dry land appear, on which the people walk to freedom.[6]

On New Year's Day, the day on which dry land appeared, 'the world was made'. And if, according to the first version in the book of Genesis, God's making of a garden takes him seven days, this is perhaps because, like Solomon (who took seven years) it is a temple that he is constructing. According to this line of thought, there was no need, on return from exile, to rebuild the temple in Jerusalem, for 'Thus says the Lord: "Heaven is my throne and the earth my footstool; what is the house that you would build for me?"' And, in the end, God's radiant indwelling of the world is so complete, so intimate, that God himself is said to be the temple of the finished garden city.[7]

Heaven may not need a temple, but it still contains a throne, for the finishing of God's creation is a royal victory, the final conquering of the threat of chaos. Hence, at the feast at which all tears are wiped away, and pain and mourning ended, 'the sea' will be 'no more'. But the manner of God's victory subverts all martial metaphors, for the king who crossed the brook into the garden seemed almost to drown in the dark waters: even in heaven, the Lamb stands as if slain. On the day in which the world is made and dry land appears, the Lord is crucified.[8]

Water stands for death, destruction, chaos. But water also stands for life, fertility, the Spirit's gift. Gardening calls for irrigation, the supply of fresh, sweet, water. In Ezekiel's vision, it is from God's temple that the river flows which turns the Dead Sea fresh until it swarms with fish, the river on whose bank grows the tree of life, with healing leaves. In the finished garden city which, as we have seen, needs no particular temple, the river flows directly from the throne of God and of the Lamb from whose pierced heart the living waters of the Spirit irrigate 'the thirsty land', transforming those who 'pour [themselves] out for the hungry, and satisfy the desire of the afflicted' into a 'watered garden, like a spring of water, whose waters fail not'.[9]

Shortly before his death in 1160, Peter the Lombard completed what was to become by far the most influential theological textbook of the Middle Ages: the *Sentences*, a collection of patristic glosses on biblical texts. The material was ordered in four books which dealt, respectively, with the doctrine of God's Trinity, creation and sin, incarnation and the virtues, sacraments and the 'four last things'.

A hundred years later, the young Thomas Aquinas published his *Commentary on the Sentences*, on which he had been lecturing for several years. In a short prologue, he wove together the themes of all four volumes by meditating on three verses from Ecclesiasticus: 'I, wisdom, have poured out rivers. I, like a brook out of a river of a mighty water; I, like a channel of a river and like an aqueduct, came out of paradise. I said: I will water my garden of plants, and I will water abundantly the fruits of my meadow.'[10]

The 'rivers' of which Wisdom speaks Aquinas interprets as referring to the 'flow of the eternal procession whereby the Son proceeds from the Father and the Holy Spirit from both'. Only with the coming of the Son, through whom all things are made, were these deep waters, which had always been at work, brought out into the open, for our delight. 'Paradise', from which the Son comes like a 'brook', or 'aqueduct', into the dry 'valley of our misery', is the Father's glory. The 'garden of plants' is the church, the tents of Israel 'like gardens beside a river', through which we are led towards the watered orchard of eternal life, of which the Song of Solomon says: 'Let my beloved come to his garden, and eat its choicest fruits.'[11]

Modern biblical scholarship adds a nice twist to Aquinas' allegory. We are now told that the voice, in the three verses which he used, is not that of divine Wisdom, which was heard in the long poem ending at the verse before, but is rather that of the poet, the sage whose human wisdom is but some small share derived from God's – a mere 'brook' or 'channel' flowing from God's 'mighty water'. Moreover, in the modern versions, this brook or rivulet flows not *from* but *into* the garden which it irrigates. But this is not the first occasion on which we have discovered that God's garden, made 'in the beginning', does not lie behind us, but ahead of us, in hope, and, in the meantime, all around us as our place of work.[12]

Notes

I. Amen

1. Deuteronomy 27.9–10, 15.
2. Nehemiah 5.13.
3. Revelation 19.1–4.
4. I Corinthians 14.16.
5. Isaiah 65.16; Revelation 3.14.
6. II Corinthians 1.19–20, 22.

II. Short Words and Endless Learning

1. Romans 9.28; cf. Isaiah 10.23.
2. Romans 9.28. See Origen, *Commentary on Romans*, Bk. 7, Ch. 19 (*PG* 14, 1154).
3. Jude 3.
4. See, for example, Karl Rahner, 'Epilogue: Brief Credal Statements', to *Foundations of Christian Faith*, Crossroad Publishing Company and Darton, Longman and Todd 1978, 448–61.
5. Rahner, *Foundations*, 449.
6. Philippians 2.11; Acts 2.36.
7. See Nicholas Ayo, *The Creed as Symbol*, University of Notre Dame Press 1989, 12; J.N.D. Kelly, *Early Christian Creeds*, Longmans Green 1950, 102–11; Henri de Lubac, *La Foi Chrétienne, Essai sur la Structure du Symbole des Apôtres*, Aubier, Paris 1969, 61.
8. On Luther's Catechism, see Philip Schaff, *The Creeds of Christendom*, Vol. III, Harper 1919, 79.
9. The custom of the Catholic authorities, since the time of Trent, from time to time to issue fresh versions of the Creed which append to it a list of items of belief, or general expressions of ecclesial loyalty, is much to be deplored. It actively invites misunderstanding of what it means to confess belief in God. The most recent fostering of this

confusion (for its subtle distinction between 'I believe in one God', '*Credo in unum Deum*', and 'I [also] believe everything', '*credo ea omnia*', will be lost on many users) is the 'Profession of Faith' produced by the Holy Office, in somewhat curious circumstances, in 1989.

III. Believing in God

1. The translation of the Apostles' Creed with which I am working is that provided by the International Consultation on English Texts, *Prayers We Have in Common*, Fortress Press [2]1975.

2. John Henry Newman, *Parochial and Plain Sermons*, Vol. 1, London 1868, 191.

3. See Wilfred Cantwell Smith, *Faith and Belief*, Princeton: Princeton University Press 1979.

4. John Henry Newman, *The Letters and Diaries of John Henry Newman*, Vol. 12, ed. Charles Stephen Dessain, Thomas Nelson 1962, 168.

5. My somewhat free translation of '*Quid est ergo credere in eum? Credendo amare, credendo diligere, credendo in eum ire, et ejus membris incorporari*' (*Commentary on John*, xxix [*PL* 35, 1631]). See also *Sermon* cxliv (*PL* 38, 788) and, for some of Augustine's uses of the threefold distinction pulled together in a form which had much influence, Peter Lombard, *Sentences*, Bk. III, Distinction 23, chapter 4. For Aquinas, see *Summa Theologiae*, IIa IIae, 1, 1; 2, 2.

6. See Ambrose, *Explanatio Symboli*, 8 (*Sources Chrétiennes*, 25 bis). de Lubac discusses at length the history of the legend: see *La Foi Chrétienne*, 19–53.

7. See Karl Rahner, 'Theos in the New Testament', *Theological Investigations*, Vol. 1, Crossroad Publishing Company and Darton, Longman and Todd 1961, 79–148.

8. Rahner, 'Theos', 146, his stress.

9. Ibid., 138.

10. Augustine, *The Trinity*, introduction, translation and notes by Edmund Hill, New City Press, New York 1991, Bk I, 8.

11. Rahner, 'Theos', 146.

12. Augustine, *The Trinity*, Bk V, 10.

13. Augustine, *The Trinity*; Hill, editor's note, 188.

14. John Henry Newman, *The Philosophical Notebook of John Henry Newman*, ed. Edward Sillem, Vol. II, Nauwelaerts, Louvain 1970, 105. For the most part, I cannot see that we need do more than say, as

we have always done, that the Father is God, the Son is God, the Spirit is God, and that these three are one God. And when, from time to time, some greater technical or formal precision is required, then I would opt (with Rahner) for 'mode' or 'manner' of 'subsisting' or (with Barth) for 'mode' or 'manner' of 'being'. And this proposal is not 'modalist', because we are not speaking merely of appearances or episodes, but of the three ways in which one God exists.

IV. Producing

1. Tatian, *Oratio Adversus Graecos* (*PG*, 6, 813).
2. On the historical issues, see J.N.D. Kelly, *Early Christian Creeds*, Longmans Green 1950.
3. See Aquinas, *Summa Theologiae*, 1a, 45, 6.
4. Gen. 1.1.
5. See Stephen Hawking, *A Brief History of Time: From the Big Bang to Black Holes*, Bantam Press 1988.
6. Hermann Brück, 'Astrophysical Cosmology', in *Cosmology and Theology*, ed. David Tracy and Nicholas Lash, *Concilium* 166, 1983, 45; Whittaker quoted by Brück, p. 47.
7. Quoted by Brück, 47.
8. Hawking, *Brief History*, 136.
9. That the first creation story in the Book of Genesis, 'properly understood ... cannot be invoked in support of the developed Jewish, Christian, and Muslim doctrine of *creatio ex nihilo*' (121) is a central theme in Jon D. Levenson's marvellously lucid learned study, *Creation and the Persistence of Evil. The Jewish Drama of Divine Omnipotence*, Harper and Row 1985. That first story, the opening verse of which is best taken as 'When God began to create the heavens and the earth', is 'not about the banishment of evil, but about its control' (ibid., 121, 127). Near the heart of Levenson's argument is the insistence that the exercise of God's almightiness is not uncostly nor is our faith in it without 'enormous risk' (156). One small blemish: he does tend to assume that doctrines of creation out of nothing necessarily make empirical claims concerning the initial conditions of the material world (see, e.g., xiii, 12.)
10. Isaiah 11.9.
11. Paul Davies, *Superforce: the Search for a Grand Unified Theory of Nature*, Unwin 1984, 168; quoted from Mary Midgley, 'Fancies about Human Immortality', *The Month*, ccli, 1990, 462. Dr Midgley's fascinating paper was read to a meeting of the Catholic Theological

Association of Great Britain on 'Creation', in Leeds, in September 1990.
12. Genesis 1.1.
13. Matthew 27.45.
14. Luke 11.1–2.
15. See n. 1.
16. Hosea 11.1–4; Romans 8.29.
17. See Ezekiel 34.16, Luke 15.11–32.
18. Romans 8.22–23, 15–17, 26; see Genesis 3.14–19.
19. Isaiah 26.17; John 16.21–22.
20. See Augustine, *The Trinity*, Bk. X. 5,7 (Hill, 291–2).
21. John 5.19; Augustine, *The Trinity*, Bk. ii.3 (Hill, 99, my stress); Augustine, *In Joann. Ev.* (CCSL, 36), xxi, 4.
22. See Isaiah 40; Genesis 2.4; 5.1; 6.9, 10.1, 11.27.
23. See Colossians 1.15–20; Hebrews 1.3; John 1.1–18.

V. Appearing

1. See Chapter II, 7, 16.
2. E.g., Acts 4.10; 1 Corinthians 8.6; I Timothy 6.13–14; see Kelly, *Early Christian Creeds*, 144–6.
3. John Ashton, *Understanding the Fourth Gospel*, Clarendon Press 1991, p. 373.
4. See Kelly, *Creeds*, 376–7.
5. Joseph Ratzinger, *Introduction to Christianity*, Crossroad Publishing Company 1969, 208.
6. See Max Thurian's lucid exposition, in *Mary, Mother of the Lord, Figure of the Church*, Faith Press 1963.
7. Raymond E. Brown, *The Virginal Conception and Bodily Resurrection of Jesus*, Paulist Press 1973, 32.
8. '*Quem credendum peperit, credendo concepit …, illa fide plena, et Christum primus mente quam ventre concipiens*', quoted by Patrick Verbraken, 'Les Sermons CCXV et LVI de Saint Augustin *De Symbolo* et *De Oratione Dominica*', *Revue Bénédictine*, 68, 1958, 21.
9. Ashton, *Fourth Gospel*, 492; cf. Kelly, *Creeds*, 150.
10. Quoted by Hans Urs von Balthasar, *Credo. Meditations on the Apostles' Creed*, Crossroad Publishing Company 1990, 53.
11. See ICET, *Prayers We Have in Common*, 5.
12. Ibid.
13. I Timothy 3.16; see I Corinthians 15.3–9; Matthew 28.9–10, 16–20.
14. See Luke 24.45–53; Acts 1.1–11; but see also I Peter 3.18–22.

15. Hosea 6.1–2.
16. I Peter 3.21–22; Ps. 110.1.
17. Helmut Thielicke, *I Believe: The Christian's Creed*, Fortress Press 1968, 192.
18. Matthew 25.31.
19. Howard Hibbard, *Michelangelo*, Harper and Row, [2]1985, 246. According to Hibbard, the image was 'developed from the figure of Jupiter in one of the Cavalieri drawings, and has always been recognized as more Hellenic than Christian in inspiration' (246). It was commissioned by Pope Clement VII in 1533: 'the defection of King Henry VIII in 1533 and rebellion against papal authority elsewhere, notably by Luther, may have suggested the subject as a grim warning to those who sought salvation outside the Church' (Hibbard, 240).
20. Deuteronomy 12.26.
21. See Mark 13.35–36; Matthew 24.42–44; Luke 12.39.
22. John 19.13; see Ashton, *Fourth Gospel*, 227–9.
23. John 9.39.
24. J.R. Donahue, 'Recent Studies on the Origin of "Son of Man" in the Gospels', *Catholic Biblical Quarterly*, 48, 1986, 698.
25. John 1.1, 18.
26. See my discussion of F. Kermode, *The Genesis of Secrecy*, Harvard University Press, 1979, in 'How Do We Know Where We Are?', *Theology on the Way to Emmaus*, SCM Press 1986, 62–74.
27. See Aquinas, *Summa Theologiae*, Ia, q. 47.1.c. In Latin, the question is: '*Utrum rerum multitudo et distinctio sit a Deo?*', and the answer: Yes, '*quia per unam creaturam sufficienter repraesentari non potest*'.
28. Jeremiah 1.4–5. The two evangelists who speak of Jesus' birth, Matthew and Luke, 'are interested in virginal conception as a sign of divine choice and grace' (Brown, *Virginal Conception*, 28).
29. Ashton, *Fourth Gospel*, 372.
30. Seamus Deane, in *The Times Literary Supplement*. I have failed to trace my reference.
31. One group of exceptions (five of the six occasions in the New Testament where the word 'epiphany' is used, the sixth being II Thessalonians 2.8) would be I Timothy 6.14; II Timothy 1.10; 4.1, 8; Titus 2.13.
32. See Luke 4.17–21.
33. John 1.4.
34. John 9.39.
35. See Aquinas, *Summa Theologiae*, IIa IIae, q. 23, art. 1 and 2. Actually, Thomas is not *entirely* happy with his predecessor, Peter

Lombard's statement that human '*caritas*' is not created, but simply *is* God's Holy Spirit dwelling in our minds and hearts, in case we misinterpret this to mean that it is not really *us* who love God and each other. So he settles for saying that our loving is 'a kind of sharing' in God's love.

36. See *Summa Theologiae*, IIa, IIae, qq. 27, 28, 29, 30.
37. Acts 2.7, 11; Augustine, *The Trinity*, Bk. X.2.
38. Acts 2.13.
39. Isaiah 62.4; John 2.11, 1. See Ashton, *Fourth Gospel*, 270–3.
40. John 16.20–22; see above, Chapter IV, 46f.
41. See John 1.4–5.
42. On this, see Patrick Sherry's admirable recent study of *Spirit and Beauty: An Introduction to Theological Aesthetics*, Clarendon Press 1992.
43. Sherry, *Spirit and Beauty*, 60.
44. Isaiah 53.3. On Isenheim, see Andrée Hayum, *The Isenheim Altarpiece: God's Medicine and the Painter's Vision*, Princeton University Press 1989.
45. Augustine, *Sermon XXVII*. 6 (*PL*. 38, 181); Hans Urs von Balthasar, *The Glory of the Lord: A Theological Aesthetics*, Vol. 1. *Seeing the Form*, T & T Clark 1982, 124.
46. Rüzbehan of Shiraz, quoted by Jean-Pierre Jossua, *Le Dieu de la Foi Chrétienne*, Les Editions du Cerf 1989, 92.
47. Sherry, *Spirit and Beauty*, 181.
48. *The Psalter, or Psalms of David and Certain Canticles, with a Translation and Exposition by Richard Rolle of Hampole*, ed. H.R. Bramley, Clarendon Press, 1884, 464. 'If I say, "Let only darkness cover me, and the light about me be night"' (Psalm 139.11). But, in Rolle's Vulgate text (which has it numbered as 138.10): '*Et dixi forsitan tenebrae conculcabunt me: et nox illuminatio mea in deliciis meis*', which he translates as 'And i sayde perauntire myrknes sall down trede me, and nyght my lightnynge in my delytis'. His 'lightnynge' has the sense of being freed from pain or discomfort.
49. John 12.44–46; see Matthew 10.40; Mark 9.37; Luke 9.48.
50. Augustine, *The Trinity*, Bk. ii. 3; see above, Chapter IV, 49f.
51. Martin Buber, *The Origin and Meaning of Hasidism*, ed. and trans. Maurice Friedman, Horizon Press, New York 1960, p. 129; see my discussion of this in Nicholas Lash, *Easter in Ordinary. Reflections on Human Experience and the Knowledge of God*, SCM Press and University of Notre Dame Press 1988, 210–12.
52. From an interview in *The Guardian* (5 July 1988), p. 16.

53. Rowan Williams, 'Theological Integrity', *New Blackfriars* 72, 1991, 148.

VI. *Peacemaking*

1. See Alexander of Hales, *Summa Theologica*, Vol. IV, Book III, Quaracchi, Florence 1948, 1135. He was commenting on the Nicene Creed. Hence, the four he had in mind were 'the unity or truth of the Catholic Church, made by the Holy Spirit', 'the forgiveness of sins in baptism', the resurrection, and the life to come.
2. See Luke 4.18; Isaiah 61.1.
3. See I Corinthians 15.44–48. For Paul's *psychikos*, RSV has 'physical' and the Anchor Bible 'natural'; both have 'spiritual' for *pneumatikos*.
4. See, for example, Philippians 1.27; cf. Luke 1.46–47.
5. See Ps. 104.27–30; I Kings 19.12; Ps. 29.9; John 20.22–23; 3.8.
6. I take this suggestion from John Colet's reading of Paul's description of the church as 'organ' (I Corinthians 12.19): 'The whole church is nothing other than an organ, an instrument, of the God the Spirit' (Bernard O'Kelly and Catherine A. L. Jarrott, *John Colet's Commentary on First Corinthians. A New Edition of the Latin Text, with Translation, Annotation, and Introduction*, Medieval and Renaissance Texts and Studies, 1985, 253). In the margin of his text, Colet drew a charming picture of an 'organ of ten chords', whose sound, 'without the life of charity ... is dead'. Colet, Dean of St. Paul's, friend of Erasmus and Thomas More, died in 1519. He has been described as: 'The last great exponent in Western Europe of a Christian world vision that was not in any significant way determined by the great controversies that left Western Christendom in fragments' (O'Kelly and Jarrott, 11–12).
7. Ashton, *Fourth Gospel*, 421.
8. See above, Chapter V, 72f.
9. '*deinde sancta commemoratur Ecclesia*' (Augustine, *Enchiridion*, PL 40, 258). Albert Outler mistranslates this as 'after that we call to mind *our faith in* holy church' (*Augustine: Confessions and Enchiridion*, Library of Christian Classics, VII, SCM Press and Westminster Press 1955, 372, my stress), thereby needlessly perpetuating that confusion between senses of 'believe' which I have taken some pains to avoid.
10. See Matthew 20.1–16; Gregory the Great, *Commentary on Matthew* (*PL* 76, 1154); Dogmatic Constitution on the Church, *Lumen Gentium*, artt. 2, 1. Gregory's word for 'founder' is *conditor*. Did he know

that, as reported by one commentator on Virgil's *Georgics*, *Conditor* was the name of a rural deity who presided over the laying-up of fruits?

11. See Kelly, *Creeds*, 385–6.

12. *Lumen Gentium*, artt. 26, 1; see Lash, *Theology on the Way to Emmaus*, 199–200.

13. See Isaiah 6.1–7.

14. See Kelly, *Creeds*, 389–94.

15. '*Quasi quotidianum baptismum vestrum*' (Sermon 213, *PL* 38, 1064–65); '*quia ipse est omnium remissio peccatorum*' (*Liber Sacramentorum Romanae Aeclesiae Ordinis Anni Circuli [Sacramentarium Gelasianum]*, ed. L.C. Mohlberg, Herder, Rome 1968, lxxx, no. 639).

16. Kelly, *Creeds*, 165.

17. I Corinthians 2.9; Isaiah 25.6–9; see Revelation 21.3–4.

18. Colet, *Commentary on First Corinthians*, 277.

19. Gerard Manley Hopkins, 'The Blessed Virgin compared to the air we breathe'. Hopkins is, of course, speaking here of Mary, not of God the Spirit, and the theme of what has been described as 'an idiosyncratic and baroque treatment of a conventional topic' (Bernard Bergonzi, *Gerard Manley Hopkins*, Macmillan, New York 1977, 107) is that Mary, like the blue sky through which the sun shines, lets 'all God's glory through' but 'slake[s] his fire'. This is, indeed, a conventional motif, especially in late-mediaeval piety. I mention Hopkins' poem, however, as a reminder of the extent to which Marian themes, especially in regard to the theology of grace, have sometimes sustained aspects of Christian doctrine which Western neglect of the doctrine of the Spirit might otherwise have allowed to atrophy. As another commentator on the poem puts it: Hopkins' metaphor 'deliberately creates immanence' (Maria R. Lichtmann, *The Contemplative Poetry of Gerard Manley Hopkins*, Princeton University Press 1989, 176).

20. Aquinas, *Summa Theologiae*, Ia, q. 37.

21. *Summa Theologiae*, Ia, q. 38.

22. ICET has 'We believe in the Holy Spirit, the Lord, the giver of life'. But the Latin does not use the substantive, *vivificatorem*, but the more active, adjectival, *vivificantem*.

23. See John McDade, 'Creation and Salvation: Green Faith and Christian Themes', *The Month*, xxli, November 1990, 433–41.

24. See above, Chapter III, 5.

25. See Lash, *Easter in Ordinary*, 266–72.

26. See II Corinthians 3.6.

27. See. Jeremiah 31.31.
28. R.A. Knox, *Enthusiasm. A Chapter in the History of Religion*, Clarendon Press 1950, p. 590.
29. Romans 5.5. See Augustine, *De Diversis Quaestionibus ad Simplicianum*, I, 1, 17 (CCSL, Vol. xliv), p. 23.
30. Pierre Teilhard de Chardin, *Science and Christ*, Collins and Harper and Row 1968, 80, his stress.
31. Teilhard de Chardin, 'The Salvation of Mankind', in *Science and Christ*, 140–1. For more of the same, trenchantly criticized, see J.A. Passmore, *The Perfectibility of Man*, Scribner's 1970, 251–6.
32. See above, Chapter II, 4f.; Chapter V, 75f.; Colossians 3.14–15; I Corinthians 12.12–13.
33. See Colossians 1.20.
34. At which point I must emphasize that the terms 'personal' and 'person', here, refer to what it is that makes each human being human, and are therefore not applicable to the grounds of the distinctions that we learn to draw in God (see Chapter III, 5). Most of us cannot sustain uninterruptedly the austere nescience required by the acknowledgment of the absolute difference between the world and God. Therefore, we use pictures. But we need continually to remind each other that that is all they are.
35. Ecclesiasticus 14.26–27 (*Jerusalem Bible*).
36. I Corinthians 2.13, 14; see Jeremiah 31.31.
37. See Lash, *Easter in Ordinary*, 216.
38. Rosemary Haughton, 'Women and the Church', *Thought*, lxvi, December 1991, 409, 412; see 398.
39. See above, Chapter IV, 46f.
40. J.B. Lightfoot, *The Apostolic Fathers*, Macmillan 1898, 406 (Vision 1.i), 409 (Vision 2.iv), 460 (Similitude 9.i). In fact, each time he sees the woman, she looks younger and, in due course, her originally aged appearance is attributed to the fact that Hermas' spirit was then, before conversion, 'aged and already decayed' (Vision 3.xi).
41. See above, Chapter IV, 35f.
42. von Balthasar, *Credo*, 79.
43. People familiar with traditional usage will notice that the territory of what I call 'holiness' is that covered by what once were called the 'theological virtues' of faith, hope, and charity. I avoid this terminology only because it seems so widely to have been forgotten that, in this tradition, the concept of 'virtue' was being used in two very different ways.
44. Piet Schoonenberg, 'Sin', *Sacramentum Mundi*, ed. Adolf Darlap,

Vol. VI, Herder and Herder, New York 1970, 88.

45. Exodus 20.3; Romans 1.25. In both Hebrew and Greek, the etymology of the terms that we translate as 'sin' has to do with mis-taking, with the missing, by the misdirected arrow, of its mark.

46. Hill, *The Trinity*, 262.

47. McDade, 'Creation and Salvation', 438.

48. Midgley, 'Fancies', 462–3.

49. McDade, 'Creation and Salvation', 438.

50. Walter J. Burghardt, 'Aging, Suffering and Dying: A Christian Perspective', *Aging*, ed. Lisa Sowle Cahill and Dietmar Mieth, *Concilium*, June 1991, 66.

51. Karl Rahner, 'Following the Crucified', *Theological Investigations*, *XVIII*, *God and Revelation*, Crossroad Publishing Company and Darton, Longman and Todd 1983, 166.

52. Burghardt, 'Aging', 70–1.

53. See above, Chapter IV, 42, 53f.; Chapter V, 73.

54. The context of the remark is Ivan's earlier question: 'If all must suffer, so that by their suffering they can purchase eternal harmony, tell me, please, what have the children to do with it?' The passages from Dostoyevsky's *The Brothers Karamazov* mentioned in this section may be found in Part Two, Book Five, Chapters 4 ('Rebellion') and 5 ('The Grand Inquisitor').

55. See above, Chapter IV, 54; Chapter V, 76.

56. According to Vasily Rozanov, the two 'basic ideas' of the Legend of the Grand Inquisitor are, first, that human beings are weaker than Christ supposed them to be and, second, that they cannot, therefore, be blamed for their inability to receive God's gifts. See Vasily Rozanov, *Dostoevsky and the Legend of the Grand Inquisitor*, Cornell University Press 1972, 151, 4.

57. Augustine, *The Trinity*, Bk. V. 16 (p. 200).

58. Robert L. Belknap, *The Genesis of the Brothers Karamazov. The Aesthetics, Ideology, and Psychology of Text Making*, Northwestern University Press, Evanston 1990, 139.

59. 'In the Son' may be read either, with the Latin tradition, as 'and the Son', or, with the Greeks, as 'through the Son'.

60. Deuteronomy 30.19–20.

61. See Aquinas, *Summa Theologiae*, Ia, q. 32. art. 1.3.

62. This a central theme, drawing on Augustine's *City of God*, in John Milbank's admirable study, *Theology and Social Theory. Beyond Secular Reason*, Basil Blackwell, 1990.

63. See Luke 4.18; Isaiah 61.1–2.

64. See Colossians 1.15–20.
65. See Romans 8.19–23; above, Chapter IV, 46.
66. Luke 23.34.
67. See the new (1983) *Code of Canon Law*, canons 960, 962, 963.
68. John 1.29; see above, Chapter IV, 3.
69. See above, n. 15.
70. See above, Chapter IV, 2 '... what he sees the Father doing'.
71. Mark 14.33; 15.36; Psalm 69.20–21, 13–14.
72. '*Dominus noster Jesus Christus crucifixus est et conceptus, et mundus factus est*' (quoted from Hill, *The Trinity*, 179).
73. For the significance of 'fully', the reader is referred to the learned commentaries on the Second Vatican Council's Dogmatic Constitution on the Church, *Lumen Gentium*, chapter 2, article 14.
74. See Psalm 72; Robert Murray, 'The Bible on God's World and our Place in it', *The Month*,1988, 801.
75. See Revelation 21.4.
76. See Mark 15.22; Luke 23.33; John 19.17.

VII. Gardening

1. Revelation 21.5; see Genesis 1.1.
2. Genesis 2.8.
3. In the (later) version that comes first (Genesis 1.1–2.3) the contrast is drawn by lyrically depicting the familiar disordered world as ordered, and in harmony, to God's delight; whereas the following version (Genesis 2.4–11.26) first describes (in Genesis 2) a strange and unfamiliar world, perfected paradise, and then goes on to emphasize that, although the disparity between God's garden and the world as known by us is to be attributed to sin, nevertheless God's overriding, garden-constituting faithfulness (bearing fruit in Abram's birth) is more than a match for our disruptive folly.
4. Revelation 22.2; see Ezekiel 47.1–12.
5. See John 18.1; 19.41; 20.11–17. Notice that whereas, when David, fleeing for his life, crossed the brook Kidron, 'all the people passed on toward the wilderness' (II Samuel 15.23), when another king crosses that valley, on the way to death, he and his disciples enter 'a garden' (John 18.1).
6. Genesis 9.20, see 8.13; Exodus 40.1–2, see 14.21–29. On all this, see Levenson, *Creation*, 73–6.
7. See above, Chapter VI, 118; I Kings 6.38; Isaiah 66.1; Revelation

21.22; Levenson, 85–8.

8. See Revelation 21.5; 22.3; Isaiah 25.6–8; Revelation 21.1–4, 5.6; above, Chapter VI, 118.

9. See Ezekiel 47.1, 8–9, 12; Revelation 22.1; John 19.34, 7.37–39; Isaiah 44.3, 55.1, 58.10–11.

10. Ecclesiasticus 24.40–42 (Douai); 24.29–31 in modern versions. Aquinas' Commentary was finished in 1256, when he was just over thirty years old.

11. Numbers 24.6; Song of Solomon 4.16. For Aquinas' text, see Thomas Aquinas, *Scriptum Super Libros Sententiarum*, ed. R.P. Mandonnet, Lethielleux, Paris 1929, 1–5.

12. Thus, for example, the Anchor Bible has: 'Deeper than the sea are her [i.e. Wisdom's] thoughts; her counsels, than the great abyss. Now I, like a rivulet from her stream, channeling the waters forth into a garden, Said to myself, "I will water my plants, my flower beds I will drench"' (Ecclesiasticus 24.29–31).